CHILE

GOOD STORIES REVEAL as much, or more, about a locale as any map or guidebook. Whereabouts Press is dedicated to publishing books that will enlighten a traveler to the soul of a place. By bringing a country's stories to the English-speaking reader, we hope to convey its culture through literature. Books from Whereabouts Press are essential companions for the curious traveler, and for the person who appreciates how fine writing enhances one's experiences in the world.

"Coming newly into Spanish, I lacked two essentials—a childhood in the language, which I could never acquire, and a sense of its literature, which I could."

—Alastair Reid, *Whereabouts: Notes on Being a Foreigner*

CHILE

A TRAVELER'S LITERARY COMPANION

EDITED BY

KATHERINE SILVER

WHEREABOUTS PRESS
BERKELEY, CALIFORNIA

Library of Congress Cataloging-in-Publication Data
available upon request

5 4 3 2 1

To Miryam Singer González
and Rodolfo Jiménez Cavieres
through you, and friendship, to Chile

PERU

● **La Paz**

BOLIVIA

Northern
CHILE

● **Sucre**

Arica

Tarapacá

Iquique

Chuquicamata

Tocopilla
Algorta
Mejillones
Antofagasta

Atacama

Taltal

Chañaral
Pueblo
Hundido
Caldera
Copiapo

**PACIFIC
OCEAN**

Huasco

La Serena

ARGENTINA

Ovalle

San Felipe

Valparaiso
Cartagena
San Antonio
● **SANTIAGO**

Rancagua

Quillayes
Talca

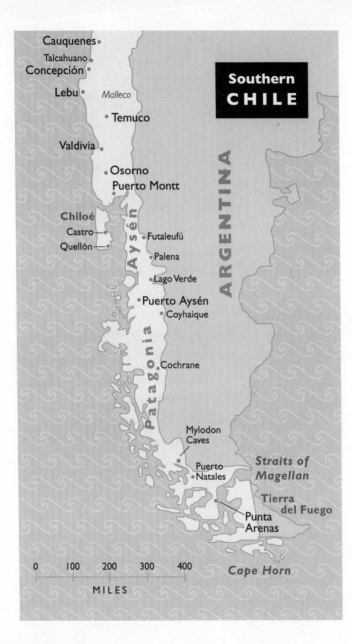

Cauquenes
Talcahuano
Concepción
Lebu
Malleco
Temuco
Valdivia
Osorno
Puerto Montt

**Southern
CHILE**

Chiloé
Castro
Quellón

Futaleufú
Palena
Lago Verde
Puerto Aysén
Coyhaique

Aysén

ARGENTINA

Cochrane

Patagonia

Mylodon
Caves
Puerto
Natales

*Straits of
Magellan*

*Tierra
del Fuego*

Punta
Arenas

| 0 | 100 | 200 | 300 | 400 |

Cape Horn

MILES

Contents

Preface

When the bus leaves Arica, in the far north of Chile, it travels for nearly twenty-four hours through the bone-dry Atacama desert—"the driest place on earth"—before reaching Santiago. As the sun drops behind the hills to the west and the mountains to the east become a black shadow silhouetted sharply against the deep azure sky, the dwindling light lingers for long moments, time pauses, twilight becomes a lasting event that may just settle in for eternity.

Chile is rife with landscapes that lend themselves to poetic tropes, wild analogies, and outlandish metaphors. The enormity, drama, and diversity of its geography may have something to do with Chile's two Nobel Prizes for poetry—Gabriela Mistral in 1945 and Pablo Neruda in 1971—and its reputation as a land of poets. Even in this age of global culture, many Chileans still think of poetry as a national sport and consider it their patriotic duty to be well versed in the works of the nation's great poets. In Darío Oses's emblematic story, *The Poet, Wine, and Sheep*, only the poet can "take you back to those places that no longer exist and perhaps never did outside your own dreams." And it is the combination of poetry and wine—another essential Chilean pastime—that drives the protagonist mad or, depending on how you look at it, liberates him from the mediocrity, emptiness, and idiocy of the new, "globalized" Chile.

This volume of Chilean fiction and literary prose makes a strong case for Chile as the home of superb narrators as well as poets. The following stories may vary widely in style and theme, but all tell tales that shed light on the human condition and exude a deep tenderness and affection for the country, the geography, and the people.

Narrative is often an attempt to reconcile extremes, forge identities, resolve seemingly intractable contradictions. Chile is a country of profound contrasts, of extremes that meet, or don't, of opposites that attract, or kill. The geographic contrasts in Chile are the most obvious: long vs. narrow; parched northern deserts vs. lush, cold south; a coastline that spans almost half the globe vs. mountain peaks and volcanoes higher than any in the Americas.

Chile's recent political history and those who shaped it and suffered it are also a Pandora's box of contrasts and paradoxes. In 1970, a slim majority voted in a socialist government comprised, for the most part, of idealists who believed socialism could be achieved through democracy and the sheer will of the people. The burgeoning of this hope in the poorest rural areas is delicately described by Beatriz García-Huidobro in *Until She Go No More* and Hernán Rivera Letelier in *The Señora of the Nightgowns*. Three years later, this government was overthrown by a bloody coup with the help and backing of the U.S. government, international corporations, and Chile's own middle and upper classes. Having boasted Latin America's most stable and long-lived democracy since its independence in

1818, Chile lived for almost twenty years under one of the most brutal, internationally reviled, yet stable dictatorships of the twentieth century. In 1992, the military government was officially voted out—the resounding No of Jorge Edwards's story, *My Name Is Ingrid Larsen*—through a plebiscite the dictatorship itself set up and organized. Again, the vote was decided by a very narrow margin.

Many of these stories have nothing, directly, to do with Chile's recent history, but the political events of the past thirty-odd years are often a subtext running through the core of the narrative or helping shape the characters and their experiences. Many of the characters are in exile, such as Patricio Riveros Olavarría's Marta in *The Ghost of the German Voyeur* or returning from exile, like Ariel Dorfman's prodigal son, discovering his country for the first time in his early twenties. Some writers don't even mention exile, but the yearning for home in Osvaldo Rodríguez Musso's piece *Valparaíso, My Love*, is palpable and deep. Roberto Ampuero's switchman in *The Train* is not in exile. He lives in the midst of it, literally, and his neighbor gently reminds him that "in this country we're all up to our ears in shit."

The paradoxes continue. In the past twenty years, Chile has undergone a process of vertiginous modernization that has transformed Santiago into a smog-choked sprawling metropolis, infected Chile with unchecked consumerism, and threatens to exhaust much of its natural resources. Nonetheless, Chile remains a strongly traditional, stratified, politically polarized society with a rigid class structure and severe economic inequities. Though abortion and divorce are still illegal and the Catholic Church retains a strong hold over Chile's social and cultural life, Pedro Lemebel's novel *The Queen of the Corner* and his collections of urban chronicles that document the marginal world of the most derided members of Chilean society—homosexuals and transvestites whose very existence challenges the dominant *machista* culture—are best-sellers and critically acclaimed even by the mainstream press.

Racially, Chile's population is relatively homogeneous, mostly of European descent with sprinklings of indigenous blood. Small indigenous communities still exist in the far north where annual religious festivals—Catholic by name but deeply imbued with native rites and imagery—as described by Patricio Riveros Olavarría in *The Ghost of a German Voyeur,* are still held. Semiautonomous indigenous communities can also be found in the region near Temuco, known as the Araucania region, where they continue to struggle, now against the "forces of progress," for their mere existence. The extermination of the native population in the nineteenth and early twentieth centuries was often deliberate and methodical, and always brutal. In Patricio Manns's *A Lone Horseman* the encounter between Europeans and the native peoples in Tierra del Fuego is rendered personal and poignant, a stripped-down tale set in a stark land and told with sumptuous words and images. The exploitation of the *Selknam* indians is descried in José Miguel Varas's *Pikinini,* in which a mother's cry for her child is the vehicle through which the native, considered by most settlers as little more than an animal, becomes a human being. These two stories offer variations on the theme of Jules Popper, the famous explorer, gold digger, and Indian killer, who is discussed at some length by Bruce Chatwin in his book *In Patagonia.*

One may well wonder what has kept Chile together all these years, why the backbone of America, as the country is often called, hasn't snapped, especially as its belly grows more rotund with each passing day: the Santiago metropolitan area now has more than five million inhabitants. Perhaps it is the attraction of opposites that imply and require one another, the apparent dichotomies that actually signify a whole. When the old man in Roberto Ampuero's *Afternoon in the Pampa* builds a flying machine, he paints it green "like the forests of south," and Darío Oses's protagonist knows that it is the idea of the south rather than its reality that is most important for the soul.

Many of these stories are sad, their characters cheerless: Chile's sordid, violent, and profoundly disappointing recent past hovers over them like a shadow or infects them with biting irony. But Chileans traditionally appreciate *ligereza de sangre*, literally "lightness in the blood" or lightheartedness, a quality that shines through even the deepest gloom and often expresses itself as exuberance. Neruda's celebration of the Chilean forest and his descriptions of Valparaíso's eccentric characters are a *fiesta* of joy as is, in a more muted tone, Enrique Valdés's lyrical evocation of his beloved Aysén.

Though Chile boasts many brilliant women writers—some of whom, such as Diamela Eltit, Marcela Serrano, Maria Luisa Bombal, and of course Isabel Allende, have achieved international recognition—their work, much of which explores internal or imaginary landscapes, would not have been appropriate for this collection. I was pleased to find the exceptions in Marta Brunet's penetrating story *Black Bird*, about rural superstitions and the women who perpetuate them, and Beatriz García-Huidobro's oddly haunting description of the life of the rural poor through the eyes of a motherless girl. Marjorie Agosín's vibrant description of Neruda's hometown of Isla Negra is an homage to the geography as well as the inspiration of this great poet.

José Donoso once said that there weren't any "true women" in the fiction of the Latin American literary boom of the 1960s and '70s. One of the truest female characters in this collection is Pedro Lemebel's "Queen of the Corner"—not a woman at all, but a *maricón* or "faggot" in the best Latin American tradition, a character who embodies a deeper femininity, perhaps humanity, against which traditional assumptions about gender differences and the values they imply, gratefully wither.

Without exception, every writer, agent, and editor with whom I had contact treated me with the best of Chilean warmth, hospitality, and generosity. Specifically I wish to thank Darío Oses for introducing me to the work of some of the lesser-known writers in this volume; and to Antonio Skármeta, Ariel Dorfman, and Jorge Edwards for taking time out of their busy lives to answer my questions, recommend possible contributors, and encourage me in my endeavor. Gratitude to Francisco Mena for our friendship and his invaluable help, and of course to Dave Peattie of Whereabouts Press, without whom no traveler would have a literary companion.

Katherine Silver

The Poet, Wine, and Sheep

Darío Oses

With their dark silence, wine and poetry can answer
any question you might ask them
                                      —Jorge Teillier, *Deaths and Miracles*

There are no *pudúes,* no guanacos, no ostriches, and
the seals do not congregate along the coast
                                      —Jorge Teillier, *Chronicles of a Foreigner*

NOBODY HAS YET BEEN ABLE to understand the
defiant attitude adopted by Cardenio Arancibia when
Lanera Austral Textiles was privatized. It turned out to be
a waste of time, a rebellion without a cause, the only outcome of which was Cardenio's own demise.

If I so boldly offer my personal opinion, it is because I
knew him well. For eight years, we shared an office and
many a bar table. Cardenio was one of those people who
could spend a whole night drinking, then arrive punctually
and contrite the following morning to punch his card, fol-

DARÍO OSES *(1949–) was born in Santiago and is currently
director of the library and archives of the Pablo Neruda Foundation.
He has won some of Chile's most prestigious literary awards for his eight
novels and many short stories, which have been published in collections
and anthologies. He lives in Santiago with his wife and two children.*

low instructions, and carry out his duties while showing almost reverential respect for his superiors. When he was healthy—in mind and body—he seemed to spend his life asking forgiveness for being such a nobody. That's why it was so surprising that after privatization he actually had the courage to spit on the manager. One could say that he did it because he was drunk, and that would also be true. But the accuracy of his aim would indicate that he had full control over his faculties. He hit Arteaga right between the eyes. As the wad disintegrated, it slid like a melting snowflake down his face and halted when it reached his mustache. Arteaga wiped his face with the impeccably clean handkerchief he carried in the breast pocket of his jacket, recovered his managerial dignity, and was about to initiate repressive action, when he saw Cardenio already floating through space.

Privatization, it's true, had left us all a little up in the air. From one day to the next, the staff had been drastically reduced. Old friends and enemies said good-bye forever. A select few continued in the company, but we lost everything: seniority, tenure, training allowances, and death benefits. If any of our female coworkers had managed to hold on to their virginity, they surely would have lost that too. We were rehired with reduced salaries. But one must give Arteaga credit as a grand master; the way he handled things, we ended up accepting everything with big smiles on our faces.

"We're going to start from zero," he lectured us. "Don't worry if you earned more yesterday. The past doesn't exist. Erase it. The important thing is the opportunity this modern, dynamic company is giving you to grow with it from the bottom up."

Everybody, except Cardenio, went along with Arteaga. We were like kids excited by the arrival of the latest, most advanced computers.

"Today, we begin a new stage in our history," Arteaga declared. "We are no longer a small local company but are now connected to the entire world. We have embarked on the process of globalization."

"Fuck globalization," Cardenio whispered. "I don't give a shit about the world, I only care about the village."

Luckily the manager did not overhear this heresy.

I remember that we celebrated with champagne when Arteaga announced that Lanera Austral Textiles had produced twice as much with only half the staff, thereby ranking among the most productive companies; that it had begun to expand into other areas; and that a subsidiary, Patagonia Lumber, was already operational and would begin to harvest the huge forests of *lenga,* or White Oak.

Every time Arteaga made one of his triumphant announcements, Cardenio hid his skeptical expression behind the pages of old issues of *Peneca, Ecran, En Viaje,* and other magazines he got from the poet. That's how he became more and more isolated. Nobody excluded him from the office euphoria; he marginalized himself because he wanted to. Arteaga invited us all to pray at the altar of his messianic enterprise. When the company rose a point above the competition, we were as excited as if our soccer team had scored a goal. Cardenio, on the other hand, remained sad and disinterested, and that's probably what led him to drink more than usual. But it wasn't alcohol that pushed him into the abyss. Nor was it poetry, which he had always liked. It was the two of them together—poetry soaked in wine.

Once I accompanied him to the Union Bar on Nueva
York Street between the Alameda and Moneda. That's where
he would go to meet the poet. He spent afternoons, evenings,
and nights getting drunk with that thin, wise man who had
the air of a saint, whose movements were slow and measured,
and whose skin was flushed with wine's reddish glow.

The poet was more seductive than Arteaga. As we drank
one glass of wine after another, he engaged us in conversation that transformed that bar into the most ancient and
welcoming tavern in the world. The poet took you back to
places that no longer exist and perhaps never did outside
your own dreams; to villages where the rain invites you to
seek refuge in a house made of aged wood, a kitchen scented
with flavored brandy, fruit preserves, and firewood that feeds
the great iron stove. His conversation carried you to a bed-
chamber buried in the depths of the house where one could
hear the comforting sound of the rain pouring down on the
tin roof, where still one hears the mystery of a good-bye
sown by the train, as the tango says. Yes, to drink a glass of
wine at the poet's table was to conjure up the mill town, carts
loaded with wheat, and grandmother's apron stained with
blackberry jam, the scent of new notebooks, the first day of
class. The poet brought back sensations of a time when the
world was made up of familiar, intimate things: books, bedside tables, and overcoats where you slowly deposited the
story of your life; scratches on the veneer of a table or book-
shelf where you inscribed the details of your days. The poet
also invoked memories of triumphant and accursed boxers,
old comic book heroes, black-and-white films starring leading men with greased back hair and vaporous tramps, tango
singers whose voices cut a path through the dusty grooves
of an old seventy-eight.

That night, I understood Cardenio's fascination. We walked out onto the Paseo Ahumada. It was late at night, and squat vehicles equipped with huge trunks drove around sucking up the garbage.

"The street sweepers with brooms made of palm branches have disappeared," Cardenio observed. "One day, these machines are going to vacuum up the pigeons, the shoeshine boys, the drunkards, and the whores. Then the streets will be clean and Arteaga will be able to walk down them without dirtying his shoes."

"Arteaga loves you," I told him, and this made him uncomfortable.

"Don't bullshit me," he said.

"It's true. He takes a special interest in you. He would like you to come back into the fold, like the prodigal son, start playing tennis instead of getting drunk."

"Why tennis?"

"Because he respects your individuality. He realizes that you aren't like the rest of the guys, that you wouldn't want to play soccer. Did you know he is determined to get people to play more sports? He says it is the best way to prevent alcoholism. He already bought us shirts and socks; we just have to provide the pants and the shoes."

"I'm only interested in playing dominoes with the poet."

"Be careful, Cardenio," I warned him. "The poet's world is marvelous, but it vanishes the moment you step out into the street."

The other thing that may have happened to Cardenio is that an animal took possession of him. Somewhere I read that primitive hunters identified with their prey; they wore their skins, dressing up as the animals they killed, and established some kind of secret pact with them. Now, because there aren't any more hunters, there must be a lot of animal spirits hanging around unattached and one of them, taking advantage of the holes in the soul up opened by wine and poetry, must have snuck into Cardenio. There's no other way to explain his sudden obsession with those quadrupeds that have almost disappeared from the face of the earth. He had never before shown any interest in animals. He lived in a small apartment with no dog to bark, no cat for him to scratch, without even a canary that could sing him a song. I think the only sheep he ever saw was the one roasting on the grill at one of those memorable barbecues the company held to celebrate its anniversary.

Not one of the employees from here, the main office of Lanera Austral Textiles in Santiago, had ever seen, in real life, those tremendous flocks of sheep in the pictures on the company calendars. I'd like to go to Magellan Province in Patagonia. When I said this to Cardenio he told me that it wasn't worth the effort, that the far south might have once been our true home, but that now they had destroyed everything, and only poetry had the power to reconstruct it and invite us to inhabit it.

One day after lunch—that time of day when you'd give anything for a cat nap—I realized that Cardenio's craziness was becoming dangerous. It was hot, and I was nodding off over some computer printouts; Cardenio yawned and yawned. We were all starting to yawn, and I told him to stop. Then I saw that he had dark rings under his eyes.

"Weekends are made for partying. 'Alcoholidays,' as the gringos call them. But on weekdays, you've got to take it easy," I told him, trying to be nice about it.

He confessed that he was suffering from insomnia, that he couldn't sleep at all.

"Try counting sheep," I suggested jokingly.

"There are so many," he answered seriously. "I can't count them all. They fill up the landscape, they spill out of their pens, and wherever they go they destroy the pampa. They trample over and devour even the memories of the land, you understand?"

"I don't understand anything. But it sounds like you're dreaming so you must be sleeping."

"I'm telling you, I don't sleep, not a wink. The minute I close my eyes, all I see is sheep. I also see the others. . . ."

"What others?"

"The animals that were there before the tundra was turned into a desert of wool. The poet—he knows all about it—told me that they were a species of American Camelidae, relatives of the camels of Asia and Africa. He also said that they have cushions on their feet so they don't damage the earth. And it's true. I've seen them. They almost blend into the landscape, they walk without making a sound, almost without touching the ground; they have big, gentle eyes and long eyelashes; they are distinguished creatures, and when they stretch out their long necks they look down and contemplate the kingdom they have lost. They are like ghosts of exiled princes, and they seem to want to talk to me."

"Listen, booze is making you delirious. I'm really starting to worry about you. Why don't you just quit, go cold turkey?"

"Listen: sheep walk close to the earth, they crowd together, push against one another, live all compressed. They get fed so we can shear them. Sheep are vulgar, pathetic, and sad, just like us."

"Who are you calling vulgar? Your grandmother is vulgar."

"If you could only see the others, if you could watch how they walk, how they seem to scrutinize the entire tundra in one glance, if only you could admire their regal nobility, then you'd realize how common sheep are."

Cardenio went on and on. I buried myself in my work. I wasn't in the mood to listen to his nonsense. The following days he came to work unshaven, after spending more sleepless nights. The smell of wine oozed out of his pores. His yawns became longer and longer and showed off his red-stained mouth. He railed on and on against sheep. He was turning into a bothersome drunk. Even so, I continued, more than ever, to try to help him, to take care of him. Because the more he drank, the more like a handicapped child he became, innocent and awkward.

"You're risking your job," I told him one afternoon. "For better or for worse, the sheep are our employers." He answered me with some lines of poetry that he had learned by heart from one of the required high-school reading books. I think it was from *Fuenteovejuna, The Well of Sheep*, by Lope de Vega.

The last thing I did for him was to take up a collection from the staff. Arteaga gave more than anybody because he really was worried about Cardenio. We paid for a treatment program at a very good psychiatric clinic.

"Don't take this the wrong way," I told him. "We want to help you. You've got to admit you've been acting pretty strangely."

He left me standing there, holding the voucher and looking like a total idiot in front of the whole office. He didn't even look at me. He was staring at the photograph on the wall of a flock of sheep with the rays of the setting sun shining off their woolly loins, but he seemed to be looking at the mountains in the background.

"They killed them," he said quietly. "They crushed their home with their inhabitants, their animals, and their trees. . . . Even here we are being trampled by sheep."

If it all had stayed between the two of us, maybe nothing more serious would have happened. But the contempt Cardenio insisted on expressing toward sheep reached the ears of the manager, who began to lose his patience.

One day, Arteaga caught Cardenio reading during office hours. It was one of the poet's books, maybe something scary because it was about a ghost town. Arteaga picked it up daintily with his fingers, as if afraid of contamination, and, without saying a word, threw it into the trash can. From that moment on, Cardenio began proclaiming that the manager was even more depraved than the sheep, that he made mincemeat of the landscape and had no respect for poetry.

"Since he's incapable of appreciating the magic of a forest, he shreds it, turns it into splinters," he said accusingly. "He turns the fish of the sea into flour and the mountain ranges and its minerals into pellets. He's afraid of words, that's why he turns them into pellets, reducing them to bytes that he feeds into electronic networks to globalize the cacophony, the meaningless chatter of parrots."

"Arteaga's mind is like the digestive system of sheep: everything that goes in, comes out as pellets, turds!" he shouted one morning when he arrived unshaven and hoarse, drops of sweat beading up on his forehead. "That's why I drink," he then declared. "Only wine and poetry can bring integrity back to this crumbling world."

The head of the personnel department approached him. He was a conciliatory old man.

"Whether we like it or not, Arteaga is necessary," he told Cardenio. "Just look at how he's helped the company grow. Don't be old-fashioned. We have to modernize. If not, you'll be the loser. Inciting class struggle and cursing the management is no longer in style. I was once a union leader myself, but that's all in the past."

"That's why I drink," Cardenio insisted. "Wine helps me recover the past."

"Try to see what's good about the present day," the old man recommended patiently. "Look at the advances of science. Don't you think it's wonderful that man has reached the moon?"

Cardenio broke out in an idiotic laugh, a drunkard's laugh.

"They send astronauts into space in a tube!" he said. "Poets have been coming and going from the moon since time immemorial, and they have given the moon hundreds of times to as many or more women. Poets travel along the silk routes with caravans of camels, and they know where the guanacos went to hide when they escaped into those mountains there in the background, when the sheep invaded. Poets can even reconstruct the forests Arteaga is turning into splinters!"

The conflict came to a head a few days before Easter. The president of the company sent us a present: a photograph of don Pampa, the sheep who won first prize in an international contest. Naturally, we had it framed and hung it on the wall. Cardenio looked at it scornfully and arrived the following day with a poster from an ecology group. It was a picture of that other animal, the guanaco, which is endangered. Cardenio hung it up facing the picture of don Pampa. The truth is that our prize sheep looked pretty grotesque. Its great woolly coat and medals made it look like some kind of nouveau riche compared to that other stylized, refined animal whose eyes—almost human and adorned with enormous lashes—suggested its close relationship to camels of the east. To celebrate his triumph and without asking permission, Cardenio left to meet the poet—who'd gone early to the Union Bar—and have a few drinks.

He returned fairly smashed around noon. Someone went and told Arteaga, who immediately appeared. He seemed more upset by the poster of the guanaco than Cardenio's drunkenness.

"Take that down immediately," he said right to his face in a pasty voice accompanied by a thin thread of smoke. Cardenio didn't move as he tried to stare Arteaga down with his blurry eyes.

The manager tore down the poster and threw it out the window. I had an image of the falling poster, the wood frame smashing against the cornice that juts out under the fourth floor. I remembered that Cardenio had said that the poet had told him that those animals, when trapped or hungry, throw themselves off a cliff in a final gesture of noble desperation.

At that moment Cardenio was transformed; he ceased to be the pitiful drunken slob that he had become. He took a step forward in a princely fashion; his step was steady and delicate, as if he were walking on cushions. He faced the manager, who appeared to be shrinking, becoming sheepish, while Cardenio seemed to grow taller until he reached a truly majestic height from which he threw out his insult.

"Sheep!" he said to Arteaga and spit straight into his face.

"Guanaco!" Arteaga replied indignantly as he searched for the handkerchief that matched his tie.

"Thank you!" Cardenio said. The manager tried to counterattack, but it was too late because Cardenio was already heading out the window.

You can imagine the rest; we work on the fifth floor.

Translated by Katherine Silver

The Queen of the Corner
Pedro Lemebel

WHAT A COUNTRY! Not a single day without something terrible happening. And not a word from Carlos, not a call, no sign of life just to let me know that he's okay. That he isn't in jail or didn't get arrested along with those other revolutionary students; because she was just about to go to Señora Catita's to drop off the tablecloth anyway and could ask if her husband the general could help. Maybe, who knows, it was possible. Full of such doubts as she hung the tablecloth out to dry from the balcony with her wet dovelike hands, the Queen of the Corner looked down and saw him crossing the street and felt her soul re-

PEDRO LEMEBEL *(1957–) is best known for his series of urban chronicles that document the lives of marginal groups in Chilean society. He received a Guggenheim Grant in 1999. This piece is taken from his eponymous first novel (Grove/Atlantic 2003). The main character makes his/her living embroidering tablecloths for wealthy families. Shortly after moving into a dilapidated building in a working-class neighborhood in Santiago, he/she is befriended by Carlos, a handsome young man who asks to use his/her house to store some mysterious boxes and meet with student friends. Thus begins this tragicomic love story between a homosexual and a young revolutionary in the days before the 1986 attempt on the life of Augusto Pinochet.*

turn to her body. She ducked behind the tablecloth so she could spy on him, watch his sway-backed stride, the lock of hair falling over his forehead, his slightly hunched shoulders as if he were a little boy who had grown too fast. The wind lifted the tablecloth just as he looked up and their eyes met. Carlos waved and flashed his pearl necklace of a smile. Oh, how she loved him, how he was capable of sending shivers of love, like little drops of frost, up and down her spine. How he made her wet and trembling, like a sheet left out in a storm. I'm a crazy old faggot, she said to herself, feeling as insubstantial as the drop of water in the palm of her hand. And Carlos knows how I feel—what's more, he's glad I feel that way. He feels safe and cozy in this house, he allows himself to be loved. But that's all there is to it. Everything else was a movie that played in her own head, the fantasies of a smitten sissy. But what was she to do? The boy made her giddy, what with his good manners and his university education. That's how he rewards me for letting him store these boxes. With his affectionate tone of voice he pays me back for letting his friends meet in the garret. And as if she needed more proof, she opened the door and in came Carlos beaming, complimenting her on the shirt she was wearing: you look great today. What have you done to yourself? She received the compliment as if it were a bouquet of orchids that dried up in her hands the minute Carlos said, you know, tonight we'd like to meet upstairs. If it's okay with you, of course. Why was he so polite to her when he knew she'd say yes? Why did he lay the old-fashioned chivalry on so thick? Did he really see her as that much older, deserving of such respect and respect and more respect? When the only thing she wanted was for him not to show her some of that notorious respect. For him to throw himself on top of her and suffocate her in his stench of a macho in heat. For him to rip off her clothes, strip her bare, leave her as naked as an ill-used virgin. Because this was the only kind of respect she had known in her life, the paternal poke that had split open her little-boy faggot ass until it bled. And with that respectful scar he had learned to live, as one learns to live with a clawed hand, stroking it, taming its fierceness, smoothing down its sharp nails, growing accustomed to its violent blows, learning to enjoy its sexual scratch as the only possible expression of affection. That's why she was so offended by Carlos's plush manners. Spoiled brat, she mumbled jokingly. What? *What*, you ask?! Carlos was taken aback. I just don't understand you. Why are you so damn proper with me, as if I were a sickly old lady, someone's cranky old grandmother? But that's how I am with everyone. Liar! It's all part of the plan. If I didn't have this house. . . . You think it's because of the house? What else then? Because we get along so well, because I really appreciate you, because we're good friends, aren't we? And if we are such good friends and you appreciate me so much, why don't you ever tell me anything? Why don't you trust me and tell me once and for all what this is all about?

She felt euphoric as she tried to maintain this defiant posture just to shake him up, break down his gentlemanly manners. She wanted him to grab her, curse her, slap her around, something, anything, rather than just stand there with his arms crossed looking at her with eyes like a calm sea. She really didn't care if he told her the secret of the boxes; in fact she didn't give a shit about those boxes, those books or whatever they were. What she wanted was to wake him up, tell him that she was choking on her silent love for him. That's why she put on this whole theatrical melodrama. Somehow the Queen had never been able to add a sense of gravity to the comedy of her flaming faggotry. She had never managed to convince anyone to take her seriously. Least of all Carlos, who kept looking at her with a stone face, a bit amused, and without saying a word he switched on the radio and turned the dial to a station playing children's music—"Alice is riding in the car . . ."—and he stood there looking at her with paternal tenderness. And with that same serenity he changed the subject. Did you know that in Cuba everybody celebrates their birthdays together, by neighborhood? Like a neighborhood gang bang? the Queen said teasingly. I can just imagine the size of the cake! I'm trying to tell you how beautiful it is. Do you understand? Sort of. Just imagine this whole block and a long table and all the little kids playing and blowing their horns. It doesn't matter if their birthday was yesterday or the day after tomorrow—they do it by the month and everybody is invited to everybody else's party. And you like that idea? Of course, there is no injustice and nobody cries because his neighbor has a better birthday party. And you, Carlos, when is your birthday? Soon. Are you a Virgo? More or less. Okay, the third? Warm. The fourth? Warmer. The fifth? Hot. The sixth? Okay, let's say it is the sixth. That's so soon. Anyway, I'm leaving you here in the house. Take the keys because I have to go out and turn in some work. You aren't still angry, are you? Who me, angry? Divas are never angry; we don't have the right to be so. And she left the last "o" of her response circulating in her mouth like a questioning kiss.

Once outside, the afternoon caught her off guard with its hazy clouds of uncertainty. This swishy-washy weather was strange for September, with one day of sun and the next of rain. How can one possibly know how to dress for this ever-changing climate? Shitty days, she thought, languid days when a girl would rather stay in bed with the covers pulled up over her ears. Maybe chatting with Carlos. Drinking a delicious wine to warm things up, smoking another cigarette in his delightful company and whispering to him from behind an I love you in letters of smoke. But unfortunately this girl had to go out, face this dreary afternoon with unshaven cheeks, looking just like a porcupine. Looking like a day laborer, she would have to go halfway across Santiago to the Barrio Alto, the upper-class neighborhood, where Señora Catita lived. Anyway, I hope she likes the tablecloth and pays me right away so I can leave and not get caught in the rain, she told herself as she reached the corner and stetched out her finger, hailing the bus with the glitter of an invisible diamond. Once in her seat, she leaned her elbow against the window and watched as the streets went by, street corner after street corner where young unemployed men with no hope and fewer prospects stretched out their listless limbs in the shy sunlight. The bus slowly filled up with workers, women, children, and university students who sat down and looked out the window, pretending not to notice if someone needed their seat. Just look at that! grumbled the woman with her hair pinned up in a bun sitting next to her. Young people these days. Good-for-nothings. They don't respect anybody or anything. All they know how to do is throw stones and put up barricades in the streets. Maybe they're not happy about something, the Queen dared to say almost in a whisper. About what? Oh I see, the poor little darlings, their parents work so they can go to the university and all they do is riot and go on strike. You don't mean to say that you agree with them? She didn't answer but as she shifted uncomfortably around in her seat, she became more and more disturbed by the endless comments of this slab of jerky hung with necklaces, with that bun like a turd on her head, ragging on as if she were talking to herself. They simply have no respect for anything or anybody, and where will it end? Finally, unable to take it any longer, the words cascaded out of her mouth: excuse me, ma'am, but I think somebody's got to talk about what's really going on in this country, because everything's not as great as the government says. Just look around you, there are soldiers everywhere, as if we were at war, and you can't even get any sleep any more with so many explosions and shootings. The Queen of the Corner looked around and became frightened as she spoke, because to tell the truth she had never been involved in politics, but these convictions rose up straight out of her soul. Some of the students who were listening applauded her and then they booed and hissed the woman with the necklaces who grumbled to herself as she got off the bus, tossing back at them a whole rosary of threats. Bah, a girl's got to stand up for what she believes, the Queen said to herself, surprised by her own ideas. Probably a little scared that she had come out and said such things in public. Then, in a swoon of feline pride, she half-closed her eyes and thought of Carlos smiling in approval at the bravery of her deed.

The bus limped along through a withered Santiago, forever renewing its load of human cargo as passengers constantly got on and off. There was still so far to go before they reached the Barrio Alto, a full hour to cross the city. As downtown approached, the landscape changed. The sidewalks in front of many stores were decorated with placards selling thousands of imported trinkets, a carnival of stuffed monkeys and plastic utensils that had put precarious national industries out of business. So many things for sale, so much of everything out on exhibit and creating a collective hypnosis because very few people actually bought anything—you could count on one hand the people who came out of the stores carrying packages that weighed twice what they should have because of the burden of debt that had just been incurred. Everyone else just looked, window shopping with their hands in their pockets fingering their coins for bus fare. But September was here, and in spite of everything, flags and other patriotic symbols hung in shop windows, decking out the urban landscape in a tricolor uniform. At some point she dozed off, lulled by the afternoon buzz. She had no idea how much time had passed when she was suddenly jolted awake by the violent braking of the bus, and there they were, approaching those green velvet promenades, clean, wide streets where the mansions and high buildings told the story of a different country. There weren't many people on these deserted streets, just a few nannies taking their young charges out for a walk, a gardener pruning the vines that hung from the balconies, maybe some old ladies with blue hair sipping cold drinks in a spectacularly manicured garden. Squinting, the Queen on the Corner read the names on the street signs as they sped by: Los

Lirios, Las Amapolas, Los Crisantemos, Las Violetas. So many flowers. I'm getting off at Las Petunias, she said to the driver, who gave her a sarcastic look as he slammed on the brakes. A high gate blocked the street, and to one side a soldier wearing a camouflage uniform stood in a guard hut and pointed a machine-gun at her. Where are you going, Mister? he shouted, looking at the package the Queen held tightly in her hands. I've come to deliver this to Señora Catita who lives in that first house. She's General Ortúzar's wife, and she's expecting me. You can call her and ask. Wait here, the soldier said as he turned back into the hut to make the phone call. When he returned, the expression on his face was more congenial. Go ahead, sir, you may pass, he said as he opened the iron gate. Very kind of you, young man, she intoned as she noticed the dark, powerful hands that gripped the weapon. This soldier isn't all bad, she thought, and judging from the length of those fingers, he must have a birdie that hurts just to think about it.

After she rang the doorbell of the enormous mansion, a voice shouted, "Come in, it's open." It was doña Catita's kind, chubby servant calling from the garden, inviting her to come in through the kitchen door. The señora is busy with some friends, but she says you should come in and wait for her. Would you like a cup of tea or something cold to drink? No, please don't bother, I'll just wait for her here, she answered, as the woman smiled and left her alone in the enormous kitchen with its shiny yellow tiles, its shelves of sparkling blue glasses and shimmering porcelain. How she would love to have a kitchen like this, so fresh and clean, with those little starched curtains stirring gently in the air, like in a hospital room. Because the truth of the matter is

that with so many tiles and that whole row of silver knives
hanging from the wall, this place looks like some kind of
fancy doctor's office, she thought as she wandered around
the spacious room that didn't smell like food at all. It must
be because the rich eat like birds, just a few finger foods,
whoredeovers, a pat of diet margarine on a crust of synthetic
bread. That was all they had ever offered her in this mansion dripping with money. Right here in this kitchen, every
time she delivered something, after traveling for an hour on
the bus, starving to death, the only thing they ever gave her
was weak tea and a few crumbs of bread served with a whole
tray of silverware and saccharine. That was it. Maybe these
people never even used the dining room. Because they must
have a dining room in such a huge house, she told herself
as she pushed open the door and got a blast of a dank musty
smell, like in a museum. Through the room's semidarkness,
the black ebony of an enormous dining-room table shone
like a lake at midnight. She felt along the wall for the light
switch, found it, switched it on, and was momentarily daz-
zled by the flash that lit up the crystal chandelier. Heavy
garnet-colored curtains hung over the picture windows, and
two rows of chairs upholstered in dark brown velvet set the
stage for a repast for ghostly diners. Uugghh, how dreary!
It looks like Dracula's table! And it looks longer than the
measurements Señora Catita gave me to make the tablecloth. I'll just have to try it, I guess. Anyway, this sinister
coffin will look more cheerful with this champagne-colored
linen. She very carefully pulled the tablecloth out of the
plastic bag and shook it to billow out like a sail over the
shining table. A golden splendor illuminated the room as
the Queen smoothed out the folds and straightened the

edges embroidered with gardens full of angels and little birds that played and tumbled in the weave. Well, what do you know, it fits just right, as if it were custom made, she mused, as she backed into a corner to admire her work. And there she stood, enthralled, as she imagined the banquet that was going to be held around this altar on September 11. She employed her flowery imagination to set the silverware at each general's place, with the red cups on the right and the blue ones on the left. No, better the other way around, with the clear crystal in the middle, because there will be many toasts with champagne, white wine, and red wine to drink with the meat, because men like rare meat, almost raw, so that when they plunge in their knives the flesh opens up like a wound. She could see it so clearly, hear the men's laughter as they sat around the table in their uniforms adorned with golden medals and military decorations. At first she sees them as solemn and ceremonious before the meal while they listen to the speeches. Then, after the first, second, and third toasts, she imagines them relaxing, undoing the top buttons of their uniforms, slapping each other on the back, with a toast to the nation, a toast to the war, a toast to September 11 because they had killed so many Marxists. So many young people like her innocent Carlos who was probably just a child when the military coup happened. From the depths of her fantasies of a faggot in love, she watched the chin-chin of the crystal turn into the shattering of broken glass and bloody liquor that ran down the sleeves of the happy generals. Red wine splashed on the table, seeped into the cloth, spread out into huge blots where her little birds drowned, where her sweet cherubim, like insects made of muddied thread, flapped their wings in vain in the thick flood. From afar trumpets played a military hymn that proudly kept beat with the laughter of the drooling generals biting into their juicy meats, savagely chewing on the greasy ribs, blood splattered on their teeth and staining their well-trimmed mustaches. They were euphoric, drunk, not only on alcohol, but also on pride, an arrogant pride they vomited out in their hateful words, in the rude flatulence they let rip as they loosened their belts so they could devour the scraps, gorge themselves, suck on bare bones and fresh viscera, smearing on their makeup like some kind of ghastly clowns. The juice of the cadavers painted their lips, covering their bastard smiles with bloody lipstick they wiped on the tablecloth. Her sentimental sissy eyes watched as they turned her virginal tablecloth embroidered with so much love into a mayhem of murder and drool. Her seamstress sissy eyes saw the white linen turned into a violet-colored crime sheet, the drenched shroud of a nation where her angels and birds were drowning. The cavernous gong of a grandfather's clock brought her to her senses and she felt a powerful wave of nausea rising from the mouth of her stomach and the intense desire to escape, to snatch the tablecloth, fold it up quickly, and race out through the kitchen, the garden, until she got to the outside gate. Only then could she breathe, or rather gulp down a breath of air to get the strength to reach the gate where the soldier on duty asked her in a friendly way, What's the matter, sir? Are you sick? You look pale. And she, without looking at him, answered, don't worry, it happens at my age, I'm not a young man any more. And she limped away, waiting anxiously to turn the corner to get away from the soldier's impertinent eyes.

Only after a few blocks was she able to ask herself why she had done that. Why had she had that fainting fit that would probably make her lose her best client? Señora Catita was going to be furious that she didn't bring her the table-cloth. Bah! Old bitch! What does she think, that I'm going to wait all afternoon while she entertains her military girl-friends? Does she think I'm her slave? And all because she's rich and the wife of a general! I also have my dignity, and like Carlos says, all human beings are equal and we all deserve respect. Clutching the tablecloth tightly under her arm, the Queen felt for the second time that day a wave of dignity that made her lift her head and see everything at the same height as her batlike eyes.

> *And this is why*
> *You saw me so calmly*
> *Walking serenely*
> *Under the clear blue sky*

Already half the afternoon was gone and she hadn't done anything she'd planned to do. Perhaps one day she would need that woman's business, and she shouldn't have let her-self be carried away by the whim of the moment. Oh well, what's done is done. The sun appeared from behind the clouds, dispelling fears of a downpour, and the city fell under the spell of that cuprous glow that drags winter's withered remains along the pavement. She thought maybe she should take the first bus that came by and get home quickly, but it was still early and it had been so long since she had let herself be carried along on the uncertain wave of an impulse. For so many days her obsession with that doll named Carlos had kept her shut up in the house awaiting his unexpected visits. Thinking about him, imagining him so much a part of herself, the street-walking, twinkle-toed queen had lost all interest in the streets. She simply wasn't as compelled as she used to be to catch the first rays of dawn while she searched for a man in the doorways of the night. Love had turned her into Penelope, the homemaker. Not completely, she reminded herself, squinting at the signs on the buses that skidded over the asphalt. Apoquindo, Providencia, Alameda, Recoleta, ah, that's where I'll go, she suddenly decided, remembering the girlies of Recoleta, her trannie cousins whom she had abandoned and hadn't even heard from for weeks. The city, buzzing through the window, seemed to get warmer as the bus descended from the Barrio Alto like a wagon loaded with human freight, tumbling through a labyrinth of avenues. Back again to The Alameda with its gray buildings shrouded in smog, back downtown with its anthills of swarming humans, back to the banks of the Mapocho River, the market with its fried fish perfume, its fruit vendors in shirtsleeves carrying their bundles in this laid-back translucent vitality. After all was said and done, it was her Santiago, her city, her people struggling between the abuse of the surviving dictatorship and the tricolor streamers floating in the September air.

Translated by Katherine Silver

Curfew

José Donoso

IN THE OPINION of those who usually offer their opinion, it isn't a style. Mere snobbery, claim the young people
who wear clothes with fancy labels and drink draft beer in
the pubs along Providencia. The usual failures and perpetually dissatisfied burnt-out cases confirm it, accusing the
growing narcissism of Santiago's Bellavista quarter of
being artificial, decadent, an imitation of San Telmo,
Soho, Saint-Germain-des-Prés, reduced to Chile's lilli-
putian scale; a den for long-haired, armchair Leninists and
marijuana smokers; an ugly neighborhood devoid of personality. According to some it was the invention of nostal-
gic aesthetes who were now trying by sheer force of will to
turn all this into boutiques, art galleries, cafés, phony an-

JOSÉ DONOSO *(1924–96) was born in Santiago. His works have
been translated into seventeen languages, and he received numerous
prestigious awards including the William Faulkner Foundation Prize
and the Critics' Prize in Spain. This text is taken from* Curfew *(re-
issued by Grove/Atlantic, 2003), which follows the adventures of
Mañungo Verde, a world-famous Chilean singer and songwriter, who
arrives in Chile after a long exile in time to attend the wake of Matilde
Neruda.*

tique shops, handcraft stores, and pocket-sized theaters: the same old story, gentrification for tourists who, God willing, will never see it.

Until quite recently, Bellavista looked like a quiet peasant village forgotten in the middle of Santiago, separated from the city by Forestal Park and the Mapocho River, cut off five blocks to the north by the hill with its ancient, rusty funicular railway. A curtained window facing the street, a door, two windows, another door, an alley, an occasional two-story house with a wooden balcony, a railing, or a widow's walk, tile roofs, painted columns, a palm tree standing erect behind a tenement, not particularly venerable trees lining the sidewalks, a domestic neighborhood of corner stores where cats nap on stacks of newspaper used to wrap candy or bread, a neighborhood that up until a short time ago offered no spectacle more exciting than the funeral processions that cross it from the east heading for the cemeteries behind San Cristóbal hill. Five years ago, Bellavista seemed immersed in the anachronistic anorexia of oblivion. The government, at that time, favored a different style, opulent and new, and Santiago was decorated with crystallized structures commanding panoramic views, to house a thousand blond families, a thousand hypothetical stores, a thousand dentists, a thousand masseurs, a thousand unisex barbers, and when that megalomaniac dream suddenly dissolved, the buildings were abandoned on their never-completed avenues, dinosaurs from another paleontological period, discarded from a sinister papier-mâché operetta.

Reacting, in part, to that failure, a certain number of young people who had gone back to wearing long hair and beards began to take serious notice of the pleasant neighborhood of Bellavista: it was cheap, it was downtown, it was old without being oppressively ancient or museumlike. The houses, with their human dimensions, announced the survival of simple pleasures, of life without tension. In the afternoon, one neighborhood lady or another would drag her wicker chair out to the front door and sit waving to lifelong friends, and in the glow of the streetlights girls would play hopscotch in the street.

Some houses were discreetly restored. Stores appeared with modest pretensions about being "different." Young people walked the streets with musical scores and manuscripts under their arms, and long-skirted girls with hennaed hair attended happenings or trysts in tenements that aspired to be the Chilean Bateau-Lavoir, or dined at restaurants a bit more chic and a bit more expensive than their earlier avatars, or were measured for vests in weavers' shops.

Don Celedonio Villanueva, an erstwhile denizen of Montparnasse, used to visit the surrealist painter Camilo Mori and his wife, Maruja, in their studio when Mori was setting it up forty years ago, in the ornate little plaza that resembled a Disneyland interpretation of one of King Ludwig's castles. He declared he'd known for a long time this would be Bellavista's destiny. But don Celedonio always "knew" things beforehand. It was impossible to surprise him with predictions, or news of a political or social nature, or even with the title of a book he'd not read. The neighborhood's destiny seemed complete to him when Pablo Neruda moved into the most secluded house on a tortuously discreet cul-de-sac.

Neruda was a great inventor of geography: Isla Negra, which many suspected would never have existed without him; a Valparaíso that was completely his, which he superimposed onto the real city, erasing all other possible Valparaísos; a Temuco where it rained as it had never rained in Temuco; the violet sunsets of Maruri Street; the yellow mimosas of the Loncoche fields—and you ended up making the boring trip to Loncoche, where of course there were no more mimosas, so *ça ne valait pas vraiment le coup*, thundered don Celedonio. Even this America to which Neruda's marvelous poetry has condemned us is more Nerudian than real—which, by the way, was what made it interesting.

People were destined sooner or later to follow Neruda to Bellavista—an ugly neighborhood, according to don Celedonio. More of Pablo's tricks! He had a talent for picking an object out of a junkman's shop—a flask in the tone of blue that, it turned out, could only be of the period Charles X, a *pétanque* ball that had been curiously deformed by use—and infusing these worthless objects with the lyricism or irony that gave them the uniquely personal stamp of his imagination.

His house in Bellavista was pure fantasy. Constructed on the last possible building site on the steep mountain, uncomfortable, miscellaneous in design, it was a secret at the back of a cul-de-sac, the house Neruda had created for Matilde while she was still his mistress. It was the kind of house where a woman in such a situation allows only the most discreet visits, in order that older loyalties not be offended. Thus came into being La Chascona, the wild woman, which was also Neruda's nickname for Matilde because of her tangled mop of hair. The house radiated her presence in the neighborhood and was the setting both for the poems of Neruda's later years and his great political acts —Neruda the symbol, Neruda the ambassador, Neruda the Nobel laureate—the house, in short, of his glory.

To many, Matilde seemed much too simple and abrupt. But no one found fault with her qualities as astute peace-keeper in the house, with all its culinary and social complexities. In those years, all the big names passed through La Chascona, always a gregarious and festive place. Matilde herself was then a young, desirable woman of peasant background, as juicy as a ripe apricot. She took long, wine-soaked siestas with the poet and was evidently related to the inspiration Neruda derived from the flesh.

The house is insignificant from the outside, in keeping with the other houses on the dead end. When you open the door, a narrow stone staircase springs up in front of you, and it is as if all the magnificence of the mountain unfolds from the first step, as if that step were a magic entrance for the chosen few. Going up, you reach the patio where the bar and dining room are located, and then, climbing a staircase made of cedar logs, reminiscent of Capri, you reach the living room and the bedroom. Crossing the terraced garden, which has a view over the tile roofs and bell towers of Bellavista, you enter Pablo's study, where he wrote his last poems.

The patio, usually cool because it is as dark as a box covered with rock and ivy, is not a place where people congregate. Nevertheless, on the day of Matilde's death, as the light faded and the mountain breeze fluttered the leaves, friends stood on the patio, the log staircase, and the garden paths, weaving anecdotes about the deceased into their conversation. But what more was there to say? Matilde had been dying, stubbornly and proudly alone, for so long! What can be said about her, except to repeat that her death signaled the end of a world?

When the boys wearing red T-shirts let in don Celedonio, envied and feared because he knew secrets about Neruda that would never be revealed unless he chose to do so, a silence fell over the company as his diminutive figure, wrapped in an old-fashioned, beautifully cut flannel suit, passed by. An incongruous note: he wore folk-style sandals and wool socks, even though it was the middle of summer. He returned greetings courteously, although he really couldn't see more than the shadow of the people closest to him. He mumbled his thanks to those who took him by the arm to help him up a stair, or to avoid a bench whose location he'd known since before his would-be helpers were born. His voice was nothing more than a reflection of so many things now withered, of the solemnity of this place that was anything but solemn. Even though he was not family, Matilde's ever-so-discreet relatives (realizing they were closer by blood but infinitely distant in life), like everyone else, acknowledged him as principal mourner.

The frayed edges of his awareness enabled him to surmise what some of these barely identifiable silhouettes were probably saying: Fausta Manquileo, her makeup smeared by fatigue, standing under the ylang-ylang, and that other person, recently returned from exile, whose name escaped him. So many people of sketchy identity who'd come to pay their respects! Meanwhile, the grim boys in red T-shirts were doubtless trying to figure out, every time he appeared, the basis for the friendship between this leftover aristocrat and poet of cosmopolitan pretensions and the man who, for them, could be nothing other than the symbol of revolution and the voice of the people.

When he reached the living room he knew only too well—the room he loved, argued over, criticized, admired, enjoyed, the room alive with stories that animated every single object and piece of furniture in it—when he reached that living room he saw the intrusive coffin surrounded by four huge candles ("real ones," Fausta insisted, "not electric. With the smell of bees and smoke, just as Pablo would have wanted it"), the old man had the sensation of entering a room different from the one he knew, a room reduced to its material reality, which was barely a shadow of all it suggested.

On the wall, as always (and now perversely hanging at the head of the bier), blazed the portrait of Matilde with two heads, as Diego Rivera had painted her years ago. That portrait, once a joke, now lacked any power to evoke the real Matilde. It had always been a bad Rivera, even if you happened to like Riveras. Today it was just plain ugly.

Everything was ugly in this dead house, because the pair of magicians, whose presence had managed to transubstantiate what was ordinary into poetry, had disappeared. All that remained was a series of inert objects, and among them the inert object that Matilde was now. The room reflected nothing more than the dubious taste Pablo had picked up in Mexico during the thirties—the world of María Asúnsolo and Frida Khalo—the hideous, crude Totonaca style contaminated by the no less hideous style of the Spanish Civil War exiles fused with sentimental memories of Capri. This house, once marvelously complex, was today easy to analyze. It revealed its more modest truth now that it had been abandoned by the twin spirits of poetry and love. Reduced to its elements, it died.

At the foot of the bier, don Celedonio, docile in the face of death, leaned on his cane and bowed his head. Three students and a blond of astounding equine beauty—she looked a little like the young Virginia Woolf—stood guard around the coffin, charged with the gravity of their task. "Virginia Woolf," whose name was Judit Torre, had greeted him by just barely wrinkling her complicitous eyelids, while he closed his own in response. He didn't know exactly how long he held his eyes closed. When he opened them, his head still bowed, don Celedonio distractedly noticed a wreath of white flowers with a hammer and sickle of red carnations making its bold statement at the foot of the coffin.

"These communists certainly know how to make hay while the sun shines," he said to himself.

Judit, of course, was not wearing a red T-shirt. But after a few minutes, the indefatigable Lisboa—yes, his last name was Lisboa, and he belonged to the "I-was-exiled-so-I'm-better-than-you"crowd; imbued with authority abroad, he now took charge here and organized everything as if it were a gymkhana—tried to tie a red handkerchief on Judit's arm. She refused it without moving a muscle. Don Celedonio closed his eyes again. He felt an annoying burn in his cornea—not even heartfelt tears. Even his grief was now reduced to a matter of form. That was his body's response to his sadness, automatic and prior to his realization that it was Matilde's eternal immobility three feet away from him that stilled the entire house. Then, with a fervor he hadn't experienced since praying in the chapel in his grandmother's house on Huérfanos Street to atone for his first and most illuminating sins, his lips automatically formulated the ancient words: "Holy Mary, Mother of God, blessed art thou among women . . ."

He stopped because he'd forgotten the rest. Even if you weren't a believer, you belonged to a Catholic civilization, to the aromatic penumbra of old rites swarming with things understood but unspoken. He and Pablo and Matilde, even if these punks seeking to change history tried to contradict him, were connected by myriad ties to that ancient prayer. He forgot to search his memory for the rest of the prayer because he was fumbling in his pockets for a handkerchief to dry the tears finally streaming down his cheeks. But soon even that need faded as, overcome with grief, he dropped onto the sofa, a distraught old man, the victim of his own memories, the last survivor of a world that, with the death of Matilde, who was so much younger than he, was coming to an end.

Don Celedonio had no illusions about his own position in that world. He had never been a star, had never gone beyond being a conduit for foreign artistic fashions, a friend of Neruda and other greats in the art world. He was a tremendous conversationalist who knew every anecdote, who had met everyone, and who had read all the books. His own writing, half a dozen *plaquettes*—uninteresting biblio-graphic rarities nowadays—meant nothing, not even as the poems of a marginal poet or dandy, the kind that had once again become so fashionable. His works were merely the mirror of what had happened in Paris during the twenties, in Spain during the thirties, in New York during the forties, and of the writing and the glories of his close friends.

To cheer him up in his moments of depression, Fausta would tell him that his collection of letters was extremely valuable. But did those to whom he wrote ever bother to save Celedonio Villanueva's letters, or show the care he did when he archived his four hundred or more letters signed by Neruda, or his letters from García Lorca, Diego Rivera, Trotsky, Gerald Brenan, and Anaïs Nin? He knew that in this moment of irremediable melancholy, when the fortunes of his humiliated country were at their lowest, when Matilde had died so obstinately alone that she didn't even want to see him, and he'd hear her voice on the telephone, worn thin by pain, as she asked him to take care of some literary business or other after her death—in this moment, weighing his own worth seemed trivial.

But how could he not ask himself the most anguishing question of all: "Did I really exist only as a reflection in the eyes of those I admired?" What importance could his thoughts on the relative magic of this room have, when it was here that Pablo's wake had been held in 1973, surrounded by a catastrophic mess of windows and books broken by savages, when Matilde's tragic face appeared all over the world? How could one imagine Matilde definitively still in the darkness of her coffin, when it was impossible to forget how boldly her cape had flown before the machine guns wielded by the "forces of order" at the 1977 trials, when the opposition carried out its first protests? It was then that this object that had been that woman shouted, "Arrest me if you dare, kill me, shoot"—and some ignorant captain did in fact arrest her and the news flew around the world.

The pretty Virginia Woolf, this afternoon more Virginia Woolf than the familiar Judit, had been replaced by a boy with Indian features, with no other expression than the square will of his jaw decorated with dark peach fuzz. In the corner of the sofa, don Celedonio fell asleep.

Translated by Alfred MacAdam

The Nanny and the Iceberg

Ariel Dorfman

FACED WITH AN ARRAY OF FANTASIES to choose from, an entire grid of streets beckoning to me, I thought I'd begin at the beginning, so to speak, go to the place where Santiago had been founded. "The Cerro Santa Lucía, you mean," Amanda Camila said. "I'll tell you how to get there. Try to climb to the top. There's a tiny theater up there, built a hundred years ago. A blind actor used to open each performance by singing a ditty: 'Come, girls, to the Santa Lucía, / Come, girls, to Eden again. / Those

---

ARIEL DORFMAN *(1942–) was born in Argentina but grew up in Chile, from where he was exiled in 1973. He currently holds the Walter Hines Page Chair at Duke University. His major publications include essays, novels, poetry, plays, and screenplays, and he has been awarded many international prizes. This excerpt from* The Nanny and the Iceberg *(1999) takes place in 1991. The narrator, Gabriel McKenzie, twenty-three years old and still a virgin, has arrived in Santiago, after a New York exile of seventeen years, with the secret hope of persuading his father— an inveterate Don Juan who has sworn to bed a different woman every night of his life—to help Gabriel lose his virginity. The only way to gain his father's respect is to find out who is behind the threats to blow up an iceberg that the Chilean government is going to take to Seville for the 1992 World Fair.*

---

without a man will a husband find / and widows will as well.' Though you mustn't go up there if it's dark, not even if somebody offers you a quickie."

"I'm not interested in widows or a quickie," I said to her.

She ignored my answer. "I mean it. Remember that the sun sets really early here in winter."

I shrugged off her warning: *"M'hijita,"* I said, "I've survived seventeen winters in New York."

I was in a moderately optimistic mood as I set off on my pilgrimage, let my feet walk me all the way downtown. It was good to be alone, a stranger in that urban sprawl where no one knew me, under no pressure to perform or lie or adjust my features to someone else's eyes and desire. I strolled along at my own pace, mulling over my list of suspects. It seemed as if almost every person I bumped into had a reason to threaten the iceberg, everyone except me. I had fallen in love with it, would defend its call for a new beginning. It was the one Chilean landscape that promised an immaculate tomorrow.

Perhaps that was what also drew the founder of Santiago to this valley so many years ago, to this hill where my short legs and my long thoughts had finally brought me. There it was, off to one side of the city's center, the Cerro Santa Lucía, where Pedro de Valdivia had, on February 12, 1541, established the city of Santiago del Nuevo Extremo. Established it, according to the Web site I had consulted before coming to Chile, farther south than he needed to, farther from his supplies in Peru than was prudent, because he wanted to lay claim to the disputed territory that was up for grabs thousands of miles deeper south, the desirable and dangerous straits that Magellan had chanced on twenty

years earlier and that led to the riches of the Indies. Valdivia
had ushered Larrea's ice-obsessed ancestor across the
Andes and situated his capital here in this very valley
because he wanted to be the owner of famous and mythi-
cal Antarctica. He left all his worldly goods and all his
Indian slaves and land behind in Lima because an iceberg
of sorts had also peopled his dreams, the hope of a new
inception. And also, according to nasty gossip, because,
being a married man, he wanted to be able to screw his
lover, Doña Inés de Suárez, at leisure, far from the cloistered
eyes of the Peruvian Inquisition. I understood him: to come
all this way just for a good fuck. I hoped it had been worth
it for him. No quickies for him on the Santa Lucía.

I stood there, at the foot of that hulk of a hill, just off the
Alameda Bernardo O'Higgins, to one side of some majestic Roman steps that led upward into a tangle of rock and
trees and columns. I stood there and read a letter carved in
stone, a fragment of a letter really, the one that Don Pedro,
the conqueror of Chile, sent to Emperor Charles V to convince him of the wondrous land that was being colonized in
his name: "So that your majesty can let those merchants and
people who might wish to come and settle know that they
should indeed come; because this land is such that there is
no better place in all the world to live and reproduce. . . ."

Well, old Pedro had been right about that: they sure had
reproduced, as I myself was proof, as all the smear of traffic
roaring behind me also proved. My parents had taken his
injunction to *perpetuarse,* perpetuate themselves, quite seriously, right here on the Alameda, my father jumping up
and down at the protest March so many years before, while

my mother waited for him to stop bouncing and take her hand and pilot her to that nearby hotel room. But that's as far as the reproductive process went. It had all dead-ended with me, this twenty-three-year-old virgin who felt mocked by the conquistador's words and the conquistador's boisterous bouts of lovemaking with Doña Inés on this very spot. Who knows if Valdivia wasn't just another of the older males in my life proclaiming that if you love the land enough you end up perpetuating yourself, thrusting yourself inside somebody, filling her with child? Maybe what he had written over four centuries ago was still valid for this child who had not yet managed to pour his hot seed into anything more welcoming than a New York sewer system.

I sat down on a bench to consider my next move—up the hill or down here among the plebeians, history past or history present?—when I noticed, to one side, a tall blond man being filmed by a camera crew. Speaking English with a heavy German accent and yet, even so, perfect English.

"This is the Cerro Santa Lucía, known to the Indians as Huelén," the man was saying. "For years, it was a dump, a wilderness of rocks and dust in the middle of the city. Until 1872, when Benjamín Vicuña MacKenna, Chile's greatest historian and at the time the *intendente*, or mayor, of Santiago, turned it into a majestic park. Over here"—and he pointed at something embedded in the rock, half-hidden by draping wet vines—"MacKenna put up a plaque the day he started work. Everybody thought he was crazy, but he pulled it off in three years. When the neighbors complained that the blasts from the Cerro were dislodging rocks, falling on their roofs and children, MacKenna didn't stop. His one concession to public opinion was to pay a bugler to sound a warning before each explosion so the people below could seek refuge. No hard hats back then."

The young blond man laughed briefly at his own joke.

"Give me a close-up of the plaque," he said to the cameraman in Spanish. As the camera zoomed in, he translated the words into English: "'To the memory of those exiled from heaven and hell, buried over the course of half a century, 1820–1872.' *Exiled* may not be the best translation, because the Spanish word is *expatriados,* which means without a *patria,* landless. Why this reference? Because this used to be a cemetery." He gave another order in Spanish: "Pan the Cerro during my description." The cameraman did so. "The whole Cerro Santa Lucía," the tall blond man continued in English. "For fifty years. A dumping ground for those who the Church or the state wouldn't set to rest in holy ground. Suicides, heretics, executed prisoners. Murderers. The people nobody wanted, nobody claimed. All buried here. A hill full of ghosts. A sad story."

The blond man was looking straight at me. "Or maybe not such a sad story," he said, gazing right into my eyes as I sat on that bench. "Maybe Vicuña MacKenna, who had been in exile, knew what he was doing. You build a park where the dead and forgotten are buried. You begin again from scratch, you plant trees, you blow bugles to wake and warn the neighbors, you clean the memories of the dead from the rocks. You don't let the past devour you."

He spoke so fervently, with such conviction, that I almost felt as if he was expecting me to answer, as if he were an angel come to cheer me up. Or a devil come to beguile me.

"You don't let the past devour you," he repeated. And then, "Cut."

The cameraman asked him if he thought that was enough and the blond stranger said it was time to go up the Cerro, start today and finish tomorrow. He looked at me curiously, as if waiting for me to invite myself along. Or perhaps as if he recognized me as well, knew me from before, from some other existence.

I said nothing.

He started up the steps of the Cerro and for one last moment our eyes locked as we measured each other, asking why we were drawn and repelled by the other's presence, the other's absence. And then he was gone, I thought forever.

I settled my butt into the bench and was answered by a sharp pain poking at me, the cassette, it turned out, that Larrea had handed me before lunch, the sounds that Chile had accumulated in the centuries since Valdivia founded this city on the edge of nowhere, the sounds that would be taken to Sevilla to entice new merchants, different from the ones the conquistador invited, to come to these lands and perpetuate themselves. What better place to listen to those sounds than here, what better time than today? What better homecoming?

I happened to have with me that small, supposedly useless Walkman that the boys of the Casa Milagros had chipped in to buy for my birthday. I had slipped it into my jacket as I was dressing that morning, hoping the people I was going to do mock interviews with would mistake it for a reporter's mini tape recorder. I adjusted the earphones, inserted the tiny tape, and switched it on: what a visitor would have to hear and learn before he was admit-

ted to the sanctuary of the iceberg at the Chilean pavil-
ion in Sevilla.

I closed my eyes, the better to concentrate, and waited
in the semidarkness under my eyelids. Then I heard, coming out of a ghostly silence, the enchanting melody of an
organillo, a hurdy-gurdy like the ones whose sounds had
swept into my ears from the streets of Santiago as a child.
I remembered how I would go to my Nana and beg her for
a coin to deposit in the cup that a grizzled monkey held as
it tottered on the shoulder of an old man cranking a song
of sixpence, a song of something lost and something
gained. The music merged into a grave, low voice, as if the
speaker were barely awake and wanted everybody else listening to go to sleep as well, as if he were trying to extract
words like minerals from the past: *"Sube a nacer conmigo,
hermano."* Rise up to be born with me, my brother. I should
have known who that was. I had heard my mother playing
a scratchy record of that monotonous voice, but I couldn't
remember the name. I had already been born once in this
place and wasn't doing too well, thank you, so it didn't seem
such a hot idea to try and rise up and be born again, and
there was no *hermano* nearby that I could tell, especially
now that the next sound made me even more keenly aware
of how lost I was—a tree crashing through shrubbery. I
didn't know fuckall about that tree; I only knew that it
seemed to be gigantic. I could not imagine its trunk or
leaves or name its species or place myself in the forest where
it had fallen, I had no View-Master to peer inside the
mountains where that tree had grown before being hacked
to the ground so that someone could capture its death on a
tape recorder. And then came raucous screams of fans,

probably soccer fans chanting words I could not decode and cheering for a team, Colo-Colo, I had never seen play, and the more I listened, the less I could identify. As if somebody had compiled the whole collection intentionally to remind me of what a stranger I was, compel me to go through the experience of losing my country one more time. And right then and there, to make matters worse, overlaid on the sonorous replica of waves breaking on a beach I had never visited intermingled with those waves slapping the wet sand was the sound of angry voices and scuffling feet and slogans being shrieked, and I wondered for one more paranoid instant if someone had indeed targeted me, was inserting this political chanting into the typical sounds of Chile to remind me of the hymns of exile that I had run from in SoHo, but I opened my eyes and took off my headphones and realized that these specific sounds of students shouting did not derive from inside the cassette but from the Alameda itself, where a straggling group of protesters were marching by, raising a ruckus that belied their sparse numbers.

They held aloft red banners and placards demanding the release of political prisoners and a rise in wages and unrestricted access to the university and death to the Yankee imperialists. All of this under the omnipresent portrait of bewhiskered Che in his starred beret, the very picture I had not yet unpacked from my bag, the very one I am looking at right now in this apartment in Sevilla. Fists in the air and defiant voices proclaiming slogans not much different from those that, exactly twenty-five years ago, on October 10, 1967, my mother and father had yodeled into the cold Santiago air, that my mother had valiantly kept invoking in

SoHo and other sites of solidarity, that we had heard on TV in the remote United States as the youth of Chile surged into the streets to confront the dictatorship. I felt a wave of aberrant nostalgia well up inside me. If I could only have joined them, if time could only have stood still, if it were merely a matter of standing up from my bench and stepping off the pavement and into the street for time to have been abolished, I somehow imagined I could reconnect with the man my father had been on the night when he first entered a woman. Maybe that was all it took, enough for me to return to the moment when they had met to understand how he had left his innocence behind, just that to follow in his wake and catch up with him. If I could only have returned to those moments in exile when my mother and her fellows in banishment sang their songs of defiance while I watched with apathy, if only I had found the guts or the wisdom to have returned to Chile on my own and fought by the side of thousands of others in these same streets and had gone on to the warm fraternizing that young cute things engage in after they have risked their lives together.

If only this and only that, I thought to myself, but the truth of the matter was that I had not, I was shipwrecked on this side of the mirror of time: it was too late. These were not the protesters of yesteryear, not the ones who had jumped up and down inoffensively, playing revolutionary games without paying the consequences. Nor were they anything like the thousands who had defied Pinochet with their faces to the wind, knowing full well how dearly they might pay for taking to the streets. These twenty-odd youngsters now parading by the Cerro Santa Lucía were isolated fragments of that mass movement, just as much residues of the past as I was, looked upon by the bystanders as a curiosity, almost sidestepped by the citizens of Santiago, intent on catching the bus or eating a sandwich or scolding a child or finding a lover up on Santa Lucía or paying the electricity bill. These dead-serious protesters in the democratic Chile of 1991 acted as if the dictatorship were still raging; they had hidden their faces with black kerchiefs, their rhymed shouts mounting in fury the less people listened to them, watched only by me, their lone witness, this solitary baby face who had no intention of associating with them. Though one girl with flowing dark hair snagged my attention and motioned to me to join her. She waved her fist in my direction, our eyes intersected, our dark eyes clinched as if we were making love in midair, and for just one more instant I had the illusion that here was the answer—all it took was the courage to take her hand in the darkness, plunge in. But I said no with my head, my face that would never grow up told her it was too late, and as if that were the sign the marchers had secretly been waiting for, their despair at being neglected turned almost immediately to violence; if the public did not want to hear their voices it would have to acknowledge their existence the hard and harsh way.

One of them picked up a stone and delivered his message straight at a bus. A window cracked and blood splattered from the temple of an old lady inside. Suddenly there was chaos: here came the carabineros swinging their batons, and more stones from the Cerro that had seen Santiago's birth, and I saw the girl who had invited me to participate carted off and dumped headfirst into one of the police wagons. I was out of there, running through the tear-gassed air. Time had definitely passed since my mother and my father and Pablo Barón and Pancho McKenzie and throngs of their friends had innocently tried to make believe that Che Guevara had not died.

I darted up a side street away from the Alameda and encountered there proof that other inhabitants of Santiago shared my lack of interest in the misfortunes of my fellow citizens: a youth in a leather jacket and tight pants was pushing a stalled car—a beautiful plum-colored Mercedes, no less—while the driver called out encouragement and a crowd of jowl-faced men and portly women stood outside a grocery store offering sarcastic advice, not one of them ready to soil their hands or stretch a muscle.

I am, all in all, a rather selfish person, not exactly the sort of guy who thrives on helping folks in trouble—the opposite, in fact, of my famous father. Yet here was an occasion where I felt—what to call it?—outrage, I guess; yes, I began to feel gringo outrage at the hostility those people were showing toward the young man as he strained uselessly to get the car going, their envy because they did not have a car, or certainly not one that luxurious. Their recommendations turned vulgar; it appeared that they were making fun of him because he was gay, or at least so they seemed to think. Stick it in the exhaust pipe, they said. Harder, deeper, they said. You need some lubrication, *mi amor,* they jeered. And I, who had just refused to join that march of protesters, decided to lend my shoulder to that young man, help him to push harder and deeper, just as the spectators were suggesting. The florid-faced driver gratefully urged us on as the crowd began to deride me as well. Hey, you can both fuck

Cara de Guagua now. Hey, *maricones,* the police will get you for child molesting. Fortunately the engine started and the youth in the leather jacket and the tight pants wondered if I wanted a ride, could they take me anywhere, and even though this meant even further catcalls from the assembly outside the grocery store—they were calling me *m'hijita rica,* they were calling me a luscious broad—I opened the back door and jumped in, and off we sped.

They wined and dined me, Oscar the driver and Nano the leather-jacketed pusher. They already had reason to like me, but their good feeling quickened into adoration when they heard I was from the States—"the greatest country in the world," Nano asserted—and from New York—"Christopher Street," Oscar sighed in the restaurant they took me to, the Enoteca, on top of Santiago's larger hill, the San Cristóbal, *"qué maravilla.* Not like here, *comprendes,"* he whispered. I noticed that he had smothered any sign of affection toward Nano, and his voice had grown more gruff and macho when ordering from the waiter: Chile was keeping them in the closet. "That'll change," he added, pouring me some Antiguas Reservas 1988, gesturing toward the city twinkling below. "People will become more tolerant as the country leaves behind its old traditions. It just takes time. The market, the freedom of the market, will see to it."

Nano immediately disagreed. They were like a married couple. He was sure nothing was going to change, because Chileans—men, women, children, and the Church—all hated gays. Ads about AIDS that mentioned condoms had been suppressed on television. Oscar looked at Nano with tolerant amusement, but when Nano's diatribe ended with a melodramatic "They want us to die," he suggested that his lover was always harping on the negative. Oscar told me how much better things were now than when they met—up on the sinful Santa Lucía, of all places. They now had a gorgeous apartment, which Oscar offered to me. If I needed help, they would provide it. "We'll give you a push in the right direction, just like you gave us one when we needed it."

Another perfectly useless person full of advice. We talked as the wine kept flowing and the dessert cart came round. And then my new friends drove their Mercedes to the very top of the Cerro San Cristóbal, up to where the Virgen del San Cristóbal, a gigantic white statue of Mary, towered above the valley of Santiago. They pointed out the landmarks glittering in the darkness, all those people down there praying to the Virgencita for someone to sleep next to. I was painfully aware that neither the Mother of God nor my own Cristóbal, my father, had been interceding on my behalf: here I was, stuck with Oscar and Nano, who couldn't help much, who wound their way down the hill and across the grid of streets we had just contemplated. Who was I to condemn them?

My Name Is Ingrid Larsen

Jorge Edwards

CELESTINO, MY SERVANT, writes the names down in a dirty notebook next to the phone in the kitchen. Whenever I take a break from work, I wander around the apartment. I can't sit for long. I write on scraps of paper, in the living room, the kitchen, on my writing desk in the drawing room, which makes me think of Bouvard and Pecuchet, the eternal scribes. Sometimes I go out on the terrace and look at the trees in the Parque Forestal, the vaulted domes of the Palace of Fine Arts, our very own indigenous Petit Palais. Then I go into the kitchen to see who might have telephoned. According to Celestino's note, a Swedish journalist named Ingrid Larsen has

JORGE EDWARDS *(1931–) was born in Santiago into one of Chile's leading cultural and intellectual families. He served as a diplomat with Pablo Neruda in Paris and as the representative of the Allende government in Cuba. He has written many novels, short stories, and several volumes of nonfiction. In 2000, he received the Cervantes Prize, the most prestigious award granted to writers in the Spanish language. This story takes place during the 1988 plebiscite organized by the Pinochet dictatorship in an attempt to legitimize its rule. Miraculously, the No vote won, and as a result, democracy began to reemerge in Chile.*

called. There is no telephone number or name of a hotel. I tell myself that I simply must buy an answering machine, but how many times have I said that?

After lunch, as I'm resting and meditating in my darkened bedroom with the shades drawn and my bedside lamp on, the telephone rings. I pick up the phone. "I am a Swedish journalist," says a thin, high-pitched, somewhat hesitant voice. "My name is Ingrid Larsen, and a mutual friend in Buenos Aires, Natacha Méndez, said I should call and talk to you."

"Natacha Méndez! Whatever became of Natacha Méndez?"

I arranged to meet the Swedish woman for dinner that night: a dangerous blind date. I did it for Natacha Méndez and for the thin, hesitant voice, or perhaps because I had nothing better to do. Ingrid Larsen was a typical Scandinavian woman: she had light blond hair the color of corn, sky blue eyes, thick lips painted bright red. I quickly scanned her body as I let her into my apartment, and I remembered something an old drinking and carousing buddy of mine used to say—good construction, nice and solid. She was wearing orangish spike-heeled suede boots that matched her pants; she seemed to have difficulty walking in them. As if she were stepping on eggs.

"Hi, Ingrid!" I said.

"Hi, Jorge!" she said, pronouncing Jorge awkwardly as most foreigners do, tripping over the *J*, the *r*, and the *g*, as she looked over all the objects in my drawing room. I own a combination of paintings from the sixties and antique furniture and some fairly threadbare Persian carpets. A gaunt portrait by Roser Bru hangs next to an imitation monk's table made in the pretentious workshops of Cruz Montt, where they drill holes in the wood to make it look worm-eaten. In other words, and to be perfectly frank, these aren't real antiques, just junk inherited from my family. Except, of course, for the Roser and a moonscape by George Elliot and another painting of a lobster by my old friend Alfonso Luco. I suspected that she wanted to say something polite about the décor and that the words finally, and with good reason, never came out. She seemed like a conciliatory person who wished to make a good impression, but at the same time she wore a scowl, a deep furrow between her eyebrows. Knowing Natacha Méndez, I thought she had probably recommended me as a notorious intellectual who supported the No vote against the dictatorship in the upcoming plebiscite and Ingrid must now have felt that she had fallen into the lair of a bourgeois pig. Anyway, she wanted to talk. They had told her I was well informed, well connected, and fairly objective. What did I think was going to happen here?

I just shrugged my shoulders. I said I had no idea. "Right now, I'm pretty confused," I said.

We drank a good-sized shot of whisky—in order to diminish the confusion or increase it, I'm not sure—and went to eat in the Bellavista neighborhood, at a restaurant called Divine Comedy. They gave us one of the best tables in Hell, a corner table next to a window, and a few moments later two well-known men entered the restaurant with their wives: a history professor who taught in Canada and who had evolved over the years from what could be called the radical left to the more or less complacent right; and a lawyer who represented large companies and came from a large family whose name had been mentioned when discussing a possible consensus candidate during the days before Pinochet had been designated the only candidate to be his own successor. The historian, a friend of mine from years back, approached our table with an ironic smile, assuming he was catching me on one of my amorous adventures. I don't have them any more, I wanted to tell him, or at least much less frequently than you might imagine. We greeted each other with jokes and backslapping—with or without a dictatorship, Santiago is a city of backslapping—and he quickly struck up a conversation with the Swede. Apparently she knew well, or more than well, judging from her exclamations and sighs, a schoolmate of the historian who had gone to live in Stockholm, someone named Perico Mulligan, whose second surname was Basque, something like Echazarreta—Mulligan Echazarreta.

"And this guy, what does he do in Stockholm?" I asked.

"Look," my friend answered. "Just to give you an idea . . . Perico Mulligan was our class rugby champion at Grange School. When he was fifteen, he had his own sports car and his house had a swimming pool. Then he went to study philosophy at the University of Chile, and nobody could figure out why. And at the end of Frei's presidency, around '69, they arrested him for organizing a bank robbery for the MIR, the Revolutionary Left Movement."

"Aha!" I exclaimed, leaning back in my seat in Hell. "Say no more."

The historian had been telling this story—a personal story with public overtones—quickly, under his breath, and I'm not sure if my companion had been able to follow.

When he left for his own table, I asked her, "And you, where did you study?"

"In Stockholm, and also in Paris. I was in Paris in May, 1968."

"So you are a veteran of the war of '68!"

"Yes," she admitted, "I'm a veteran of '68," and her voice, as she pronounced the Spanish words somewhat slowly, with some difficulty, much like the way she balanced precariously on those spike heels, skidded into a melodious laugh. Quickly she became serious again and repeated the question she had posed at my house.

"So what do you think is going to happen here?"

I repeated that I didn't have any idea.

"But, do you really think the No can win, as some opposition politicians claim?"

"The No," I said, "*can* win."

She looked at me in silence, and frowned. Then quickly said, "But it is impossible, Jorge!" She made this affirmation as if it were categorical, definitive. It wasn't a simple circumstantial impossibility but rather a metaphysical fact. There before me paraded Plato and Aristotle, as well as Martin Luther and John Calvin, and spiced up, I suppose, with Karl Marx, but only very mildly. I just smiled. I felt something like a diffuse flutter behind my ears: the whisper of miscommunication.

"So, Jorge, you believe that a dictator can organize a plebiscite in order to lose it?"

I spread out my hands as if asking for a cease fire. I picked up the fork and attacked my spinach ravioli. Accompanied by a bottle of thick but velvety red Santa Digna, they were utterly scrumptious.

Ingrid Larsen shook her head with an air of commiseration, convinced that we Chileans were deluded madmen, and I must confess that she managed to infect me with her conviction, at least for a few hours. Nevertheless, she praised the meal enthusiastically, gratefully. It seemed that being a veteran of street battles did not prevent her from displaying the best and most traditional good manners, and as she was leaving, she went up to the historian to say good-bye. Having met somebody who had actually known Perico Mulligan constituted, it seemed, a crucial episode in her visit to Chile. I had to hold her arm to help her maintain a vertical position over her spike heels, which got stuck in the godforsaken cracks in the sidewalk, and I could see the insinuating glances of the two couples, who watched me through the window.

The meeting I have just described occurred four or five weeks before the plebiscite. She was leaving the next day for Concepción, then for Buenos Aires, and from there she would return to Santiago and would call me. "That is, if they let me back in," she said, a comment I did not fully understand at the time. Since she didn't at all trust the perspective of the political circles in Santiago, nor that of bohemian intellectuals—in which category she probably included me—she had to go visit the poorest slums, go into the very heart of the heartland, attend clandestine meetings with representatives of the ultraleft.

On the afternoon of October 3, two days before the plebiscite, facing the trees of the Parque Forestal, with the distant lights of the Virgin atop the Cerro San Cristóbal, at dusk when the heavy dust of a long day had finally dissipated, she sat on my terrace and repeated the question we could now consider a classic: "So, Jorge, what do you think is going to happen?" as if before now I had not really answered her seriously. And she placed a small tape recorder on the glass tabletop between a slab of fresh creamy cheese from Quillayes and a couple of glasses of white wine.

I told her that the last time we had talked I had not been fully convinced. I thought that the government had obtained its objective of frightening people with the idea of the return of Allende, "and as you know, Ingrid, the perception of the Allende period inside Chile is very different from what you might hear on the rive gauche of Paris, or in Madrid, or on an island in the Stockholm Archipelago. . . .

She raised her pale blue eyes, where I saw the hint of a tremor, a gentle ripple over otherwise calm waters; then she focused her attention on the tape recorder.

"Is it taping?"

"Yes," she said. "It's taping."

"Now, however, I am convinced that the No is going to win."

"Are you sure?"

"If I had to bet, I'd bet on the No winning, and by a pretty big . . ."

At that precise moment, all the lights in the sector we could see below us from the terrace blinked and went out. Even the Virgin of the Cerro San Cristóbal was left in darkness under the starry sky.

"You see!" she said, in a tone that sounded almost triumphant.

"What?"

"They say they will cause a blackout, like now, and steal the votes from the booths."

"It's not so easy to rob the voting booths."

"But this is a dictatorship, Jorge! Don't you realize that?"

"I do, Ingrid," I said, patting her cheek in the semidark-ness. "I have for fifteen years."

She shook her head in a gesture of impotence, as if my stubbornness were suffocating her, and I, laughing, imitated her. I filled her cup then mine in the darkness. At that moment, the lights began to go on. When she had called, Ingrid had said that she wanted to invite me to the restau-rant of my choice. But I got out of it by pretending to have a previous engagement. Although dealing with foreign jour-nalists can sometimes be pleasant, it always ends up being a bit overwhelming. Especially when they come from the developed world. They never stop working, first of all; and they never stop pumping us for information. And worst of all, they look at us from their distance with a kind of know-ing smile, as if they were the civilized ones, who knew what was going on, and we were just a bunch of *bons sauvages*. They would listen condescendingly to our funny answers, our naïve theories, and wouldn't believe a word we said.

I waited for her to go down in the elevator, then I put on an old jacket, brushed my hair quickly, and stuffed a bit of money in my pocket. I walked slowly toward El Biógrafo, a café on the corner of Lastarria and Villavicencio. There were soldiers with machine guns in the streets; the atmo-sphere was heavy. In El Biógrafo, I drank a couple of glasses of wine and sat at the counter, uncomfortably, to eat some-thing called a Spanish tortilla—a bomb made of eggs, onions, and chorizo—with elbows jabbing me and loud voices all around. Someone said it seemed like a conspiracy was underway, but the government in Washington was going to stop it. With the complicity, they say, of one of the chiefs of staff. Will they really stop it? someone else wondered. They slapped me on the shoulder and invited me for a drink. "It's a little late for drinks," I said grumpily. "Thanks anyway."

I thought Ingrid Larsen would call Thursday morning. To congratulate me, I was naïve enough to assume, as many Chilean friends had done, and to talk about the outcome. But she didn't call all of Thursday, a day when my neighborhood was transformed into a carnival, and she didn't call Friday either. I even wondered if deep down she was disgusted because reality had contradicted her theories, but she was a good person, and there was no room to doubt her genuinely democratic sentiments. Later I learned that after the celebration on Friday in O'Higgins Park, a special police unit had savagely attacked some foreign journalists, resulting in many wounded and a lot of broken cameras. I called the hotel on Saturday morning, a bit worried, and nobody answered in her room. I called again at seven in the evening and she answered with an even thinner, incredibly fragile, tense voice.

"I'm very afraid," she said.

"Why?"

"Didn't you hear what happened to my colleagues?"

It had been a perfectly premeditated punishment, "their revenge against us." She had gone that morning to a very poor neighborhood, La Victoria, and seen a white car following her. When she returned, she noticed some strange people with grim faces in the hotel lobby. When she asked for her key, they handed her two messages from a Mr. Mulligan. Mulligan? "Yes . . . I thought it might be one of Perico's relatives, but I also thought it strange that they didn't leave a phone number." Then, when she entered her room, the phone rang again and she got scared. She was shaking with fear as she picked it up. She heard some heavy breathing, some distant footsteps on a wood floor, background music, then the caller hung up. Five minutes later, again.

"Hello!"

"Did you see what happened to your colleagues, you Swedish cunt? The next time, it'll be you!"

Hysterical, she pressed all the buttons next to her bed and called the reception desk for help. Losing control had made her lose her Spanish, and she had a hard time making herself understood. Someone came to see her, finally— a manager wearing a dark suit and a pearl-gray tie. He bowed to her and said that this establishment, Mrs. Larsen, guaranteed her security but he couldn't, naturally, prevent someone from calling on the telephone from outside the hotel and saying disagreeable things; however, inside the hotel she should feel perfectly safe. They would definitely inform the police, of course. But the hotel took full responsibility for her safety. That's all she needed!

When she finished telling her story, I told her I would meet her in the hotel bar punctually at eight o'clock in the evening. I told her to try to stay calm. Threats over the telephone had become, in this disgraceful country, par for the course.

I arrived two minutes early in the bar, a dimly lit, semi-subterranean space furnished with leather easy chairs shaped like corollas or placentas. I chose a low table with a black glass top, and began to look at the headlines of *La Segunda* as I sank into one of those soporific placentas. True to her punctual Nordic character, she sat down in the facing chair at eight on the dot. We drank pisco sours, picked at some hors d'oeuvres topped with mayonnaise, and talked. There was something, she said, that she hadn't told me, and it would explain her fear. She looked around. I noticed that she was uncharacteristically agitated, fatigued, and unkempt. For a fraction of a second, her eyes rested on some people sitting in a dark corner. She remained silent and seemed to have difficulty swallowing. She took a gulp of air, of nothing.

She had first come to Chile five or six years ago, when the street demonstrations and protests had just begun, and the authorities had thrown her out mercilessly. Three men, like the ones sitting in the corner, she explained, swallowing and touching her chest with her finger, had knocked on the door of her hotel room, pushed their way in, and told her she had ten minutes to pack her bags while they waited for her in the hallway. Then they took her to the airport in one of those white cars. Why? Because she had written in the Swedish newspapers about what was going on here— about the starving people, the jails, the tortured, the disappeared. She was not the only foreign journalist who had done so, but there is nothing more unpredictable than the secret police: they choose a particular person, for whatever reason, perhaps just to serve as an example, a scapegoat, and they leave everybody else alone.

"In addition, I did a lot for the Chileans in Stockholm, and apparently the embassy passed on detailed information."

"They don't have anything better to do," I told her, "and if you are also such a good friend of that Perico Mulligan. . . ."

She looked at me from under her eyebrows as if asking

herself what exactly my words contained. Mockery? Reproach? Jealousy? What? She looked at me, then decided she could continue. She had introduced herself to me as Ingrid Larsen, but her full name was Louise Ingrid Gustafsson Larsen, and her by-line on all the articles she wrote for the newspapers in Stockholm and on her radio reports in Guttenberg was Louise Gustafsson.

"Beautiful," I said. "A very literary name."

"Lars Gustafsson exists," she said.

"And so does Louise Gustafsson."

For the first time that evening, the smile I remembered from our previous encounters appeared on her face. Anyway, she had arranged for the Swedish consul to get her another passport. Registered name: Ingrid G. Larsen. Equipped with this semifalse document ("As you can imagine, something very unusual for a Swedish functionary to do, but because it was for Chile . . ."), and a different hairstyle, but with her own natural hair color—because before it had been dyed a kind of reddish chestnut brown—she returned to Santiago.

"I was terribly frightened, but I was determined to know what was going to happen."

The employee of the immigration police hit some keys on his computer, looked at the screen, and stamped her passport without blinking. From that point on, she felt perfectly comfortable. She concluded that the country had changed; her expulsion had been part of its prehistory. When the time came, she obtained credentials from the headquarters of the No. She then thought she would need official credentials, in order to gain access to the Diego Portales building, where the government's computer central is located, to interview members of the government about anything that may come up. So she went, rather officiously, to the offices of the National Office of Social Communications. There, from behind a counter and under a photograph of the President and Captain General of the Nation and One and Only Candidate, a bespeckled young woman asked for her passport and two photographs. Ten minutes later—or maybe less "because they serve you very quickly, with no bureaucracy, did you know?"—she returned with the passport and a large name tag full of official stamps, made to be worn on a lapel or hanging from your neck so it will be visible.

"So the special forces know who they're beating up. . . ."

My joke came out sounding a bit morbid, and she acknowledged it by merely raising her eyebrows.

"I got up from my chair, took my passport and my credential, and read it."

In perfect handwriting and correct spelling it read Louise Ingrid Gustafsson Larsen. She turned pale and felt as if she couldn't breathe in that room with all those people walking around, over which the portrait of the Captain General seemed to dominate completely, and she observed that the young lady's eyes behind her thick glasses remained expressionless.

I drank the dregs of my pisco sour, called over the waiter, and asked Louise Ingrid if she wanted another dose.

"Yes," she said, "please."

"What do you expect?" I said. "They aren't stupid."

She was flying out the following morning and now, after her second pisco, she was going to pack her bags and try to sleep behind her door with seven locks. She just prayed she wouldn't have to hear those voices over the telephone again.

I accompanied her to the fifteenth floor and said good-bye to her with a kiss in front of her door. I made sure she had a deadbolt on her door, and I told her to use it even if everything seemed perfectly quiet in the hotel. But she didn't seem reassured and kept her eyes glued on me as she closed the door. I waited until I heard her turn the bolt, then walked quickly away.

I must confess that I felt somewhat relieved when I reached the street. Those Swedes! I said to myself. This confession does not reflect well on me, but what can I do? I had planned to go home to bed, but I am an irremediable glutton, forever hungry, and instead of walking toward Ismael Valdés Vergara along the edge of the Parque Forestal, I turned to the east, walking quickly through Plaza Italia. Walking is my only exercise, and it is good for my health, at night or in the daytime, with or without alcohol in my blood. I remembered the old Parque Japonés and the young girls there, sometimes called the Balmaceda River girls (because of the statue of President Balmaceda near the Mapocho River). Now there weren't any more girls with red painted lips but rather muggers, lurking, perhaps, in the bushes, so I walked instead along the southern side of Providencia Boulevard. El Parrón, one of Santiago's classic hangouts, had its lights on and looked as welcoming as always. I crossed the street and went in.

I sat down at a table in the first dining room where a few couples were eating quietly. I placed my order—steak, a green salad, artichoke hearts, half a bottle of red wine—and went to the bathroom. Next to the urinals stood two large, unpleasant-looking men. One of them was dressed in beige corduroy pants. He was tall and bald, with a red head, and was wearing a dirty sweater and round glasses. I realized immediately that they recognized me and were looking at me with evident hostility.

"Is Volodia here?" he asked, and when his companion looked at him questioningly, without understanding, he spoke the full name of the communist intellectual and poet, "Volodia Teitelboim" in a tone that meant, "the red, the political extremist." I assumed they were pointing at me behind my back. I concentrated on my prosaic task at the urinal. I washed my hands and took the paper towel the attendant handed me. The same guy, now pretending to talk to the attendant over my shoulders, said, "Do you know when Volodia Teitelboim is supposed to come? Because it seems like they're having a meeting here." I dried my hands with all the calm I could muster and took some coins out of my pocket, carefully avoiding any gesture that might give me away. "Your tip is my salary," begged the sign, hand-written with a black marker on a scrap of cardboard. I could only imagine the looks I was getting as I left.

At the very moment my order came, the two bruisers entered the room and sat down four tables away from me. I chewed with difficulty. I tried to wash the meat down with a sip of wine. A piece of hard bread struck my ear and was followed by boisterous laughter. I got up, crossed the hall-way, and entered the bar to look for the manager, but they told me he was already gone. I also, I thought, have to go to the managers, and the managers always slip away, like eels. I talked to the bartender, who knew me and who was at his post, wielding bottles of different colors, and he told me I could sit at the counter, if I wanted, or at a table in the bar. They would leave me alone in there.

"Just give me the bill!" I told him, furious, and I went back into the dining room to get my jacket. The steak was drying up on the plate, and the salad was wilting. The two brutes were chewing voraciously and didn't even look at me. One of the waiters came up to me with a serious, important look on his face, and the bartender, from his refuge behind the bar on the other side of the dining room, called to him and told him not to charge me.

"You really should choose your clientele a bit more carefully," I told him.

The bartender made a gesture of impotence, a gesture that meant many things and carried a lot of history. "Can I offer you an after-dinner drink on the house?"

I didn't even bother to answer him. I took a taxi, because now I knew that Santiago at night was not very safe. Never, in all these years, had it been safe—why kid ourselves now? "Poor Swede!" I mumbled, thinking that she was right after all, that there were plenty of reasons to be afraid in this country, and I had acted badly, selfishly, arrogantly; and then I mumbled, "Poor us!"

Translated by Katherine Silver

-{ Along the Coast }-

Roaming in Valparaíso
Pablo Neruda

VALPARAÍSO IS VERY CLOSE TO SANTIAGO. They are separated only by the shaggy mountains on whose peaks tall cacti, hostile but flowering, rise like obelisks. And yet something impossible to define keeps Valparaíso apart from Santiago. Santiago is a captive city behind walls of snow. Valparaíso, on the other hand, throws its doors wide to the infinite sea, to its street cries, to the eyes of children.

At the wildest stage of our young manhood, we would suddenly—always at daybreak, always without having slept, always without a penny in our pockets—board a third-class coach. We were poets and painters, all of us about twenty years old, brimming over with a precious store of impulsive madness that was dying to be used, to expand, to burst out. The star of Valparaíso beckoned to us with its magnetic pulsebeat.

PABLO NERUDA *(1904–73) was born in Parral, Chile. He shared the World Peace Prize with Paul Robeson and Pablo Picasso in 1950 and was awarded the Nobel Prize in Literature in 1971. The sketches throughout this volume are taken from his* Memoirs (Confieso que he vivido), *published posthumously in 1974.*

It wasn't until many years later that I felt this same inexplicable call again. It was during my years in Madrid. In a tavern, coming out of the theater in the small hours, or simply walking the streets, I would suddenly hear the voice of Toledo calling me, the soundless voice of its ghosts and its silence. And at that late hour, with friends as crazy as those of my younger days, I took off for the ancient, ashen, twisted citadel. To sleep in our clothes on the sands of the Tagus, under stone bridges.

I don't know why, but of all the trips to Valparaíso I can picture to myself, one remains fixed in my mind, permeated by an aroma of herbs uprooted from the intimacy of the fields. We were going to see a poet and a painter off, they would be traveling to France third class. We did not have enough money between all of us to pay for even the dingiest hotel, so we looked up Novoa, one of our favorite lunatics in wonderful Valparaíso. It wasn't easy to get to his house. Scrambling and slipping up and down endless hills, we followed Novoa's undaunted silhouette as he guided us along.

He was an impressive man, with a bushy beard and a thick mustache. His dark coattails flapped like wings on the mysterious slopes of the ridge we were climbing, blindly, worn out. He never stopped talking. He was a mad saint, personally canonized by us poets. And he was, naturally, a naturalist; a vegetarian's vegetarian. He praised the secret ties, known only to him, between bodily health and the natural gifts of the earth. He preached to us as he walked along; he threw his thundering voice back at us, as if we were his disciples. His huge figure advanced like a St. Christopher native to these dark, forsaken suburbs.

At last we reached his house, which turned out to be a cabin with two rooms. Our St. Christopher's bed occupied one of them. The other was mostly taken up by an enormous wicker armchair, lavishly crisscrossed by superfluous rosettes and with quaint little drawers built into its arms. A Victorian masterpiece. The huge armchair was assigned to me for sleeping that night. My friends spread the evening papers over the floor and stretched out carefully on news items and editorial columns.

Their breathing and their snores soon told me that they were all sound asleep. Sitting in that monumental piece of furniture, my weary bones found it difficult to coax sleep. I could hear a silence coming from the heights, the lonely peaks. Only the occasional barking of the Dog Stars in the darkness, only the faraway whistle of an arriving or departing ship made this night in Valparaíso real for me.

Suddenly I felt a strange, irresistible force flooding through me. It was a mountain fragrance, a smell of the prairie, of vegetation that had grown up with me during my childhood and which I had forgotten in the noisy hubbub of city life. I started to feel drowsy, cradled in the lullaby of the mother soil. Where could this wild breath of the earth, this purest of aromas, be coming from? My fingers probed into the nooks and crannies of the huge wicker chair and discovered the innumerable little drawers, and in them I could feel dry, smooth plants, coarse, rounded sheaves, spear-like, soft or metallic leaves. The entire health-giving arsenal of our vegetarian preacher, the complete record of a life spent by our exuberant wandering St. Christopher gathering wild plants with his huge hands. Once this enigma had been cleared up, I fell asleep peacefully, protected by the fragrance of those guardian herbs.

For several weeks I lived across from Don Zoilo Escobar's house on a narrow street in Valparaíso. Our balconies almost touched. My neighbor would come out on his balcony early in the morning to do exercises like a hermit, exposing the harp of his ribs. Invariably dressed in a poor man's overalls or a frayed overcoat, half sailor, half archangel, he had retired long ago from his sea voyages, from the customs house, from the ships' crews. He brushed his Sunday suit every day with the meticulous thoroughness of a perfectionist. It was a distinguished-looking black flannel suit that, over the years, I never saw him wear—an outfit he kept among his treasures in a decrepit old wardrobe.

But his most precious and heart-rending treasure was a Stradivarius which he watched over with devotion all his life, never playing it or allowing anyone else to. Don Zoilo was thinking of selling it in New York, where he would be given a fortune for the famed instrument. Sometimes he brought it out of the dilapidated wardrobe and let us look at it, reverently. Someday Don Zoilo would go north and return without a violin but loaded with flashy rings and with gold teeth filling the gaps the slow passing of the years had gradually left in his mouth.

One morning he did not come out to his gymnasium balcony. We buried him in the cemetery up on the hill, in his black flannel suit, which covered his small hermit's bones for the first time. The strings of the Stradivarius could not weep over his departure. Nobody knew how to play it. Moreover, the violin was not in the wardrobe when it was opened. Perhaps it had flown out to sea, or to New York, to crown Don Zoilo's dreams.

Valparaíso is secretive, sinuous, winding. Poverty spills over its hills like a waterfall. Everyone knows how much the infinite number of people on the hills eat and how they dress (and also how much they do not eat and how they do not dress). The wash hanging out to dry decks each house with flags and the swarm of bare feet constantly multiplying betrays unquenchable love.

Near the sea, however, on flat ground, there are balconied houses with closed windows, where hardly any footsteps ever enter. The explorer's mansion was one of those houses. I knocked repeatedly with the bronze knocker to make sure I would be heard. At last, soft footfalls approached and a quizzical face suspiciously opened the portal just a crack, wanting to keep me out. It was the old serving woman of the house, a shadow in a square shawl and an apron, whose footsteps were barely a whisper.

The explorer, who was also quite old, and the servant lived all alone in the spacious house with its windows closed. I had come there to see what his collection of idols was like. Corridors and walls were filled with bright-red creatures, masks with white and ash-colored stripes, statues representing the vanished anatomies of sea gods, wigs of dried-up Polynesian hair, hostile wooden shields covered with leopard skin, necklaces of fierce-looking teeth, the oars of skiffs that may have cut through the foam of favorable waters. Menacing knives made the walls shudder with silver blades that gleamed through the shadows.

I noticed that the virile wooden gods had been emasculated. Their phalluses had been carefully covered with loincloths, obviously the same cloth used by the servant for her shawl and her apron.

The old explorer moved among his trophies stealthily. In room after room, he supplied me with the explanations, half peremptory and half ironic, of someone who had lived a good deal and continued to live in the afterglow of his images. His white goatee resembled a Samoan idol's. He showed me the muskets and huge pistols he had used to hunt the enemy and make antelopes and tigers bite the dust. He told his adventures without varying his hushed tone. It was as if the sunlight had come in through the closed windows to leave just one tiny ray, a tiny butterfly, alive, flitting among the idols.

On my way out, I mentioned a trip I planned to the Islands, my eagerness to leave very soon for the golden sands. Then, peering all around him, he put his frazzled mustache to my ear and shakily let slip: "Don't let her find out, she mustn't know about it, but I am getting ready for a trip, too."

He stood that way for an instant, one finger on his lips, listening for the possible tread of a tiger in the jungle. And then the door closed on him, dark and abrupt, like night falling over Africa.

I questioned the neighbors: "Are there any new eccentrics around? Is there anything worth coming back to Valparaíso for?"

They answered: "There's almost nothing to speak of. But if you go down that street you'll run into Don Bartolomé."

"And how am I going to know him?"

"There's no way you can make a mistake. He always travels in a grand coach."

A few hours later I was buying some apples in a fruit store when a horse-drawn carriage halted at the door. A tall, ungainly character dressed in black got out of it. He, too, was going to buy apples. On his shoulder he carried an all-green parrot, which immediately flew over to me and perched on my head without even looking where it was going.

"Are you Don Bartolomé?" I asked the gentleman.

"That's right. My name is Bartolomé." And pulling out a long sword he carried under his cape, he handed it to me, while he filled his basket with the apples and grapes he was buying. It was an ancient sword, long and sharp, with a hilt worked by fancy silversmiths, a hilt like a blown rose.

I didn't know him, and I never saw him again. But I accompanied him into the street with due respect, silently opened the carriage door for him and his basket of fruit to get in, and solemnly placed the bird and the sword in his hands.

Small worlds of Valparaíso, unjustly neglected, left behind by time, like crates abandoned in the back of a warehouse, nobody knows when, never claimed, come from nobody knows where, crates that will never go anywhere. Perhaps in these secret realms, in these souls of Valparaíso, was stored forever the lost power of a wave, the storm, the salt, the sea that flickers and hums. The menacing sea locked inside each person: an uncommunicable sound, an isolated movement that turned into the flour and the foam of dreams.

I was amazed that those eccentric lives I discovered were such an inseparable part of the heartbreaking life of the port. Above, on the hills, poverty flourishes in wild spurts of tar and joy. The derricks, the piers, the works of man cover the waist of the coast with a mask painted on by happiness that comes and goes. But others never made it to the hilltops, or down below, to the jobs. They put away their own infinite world, their fragment of the sea, each in his own box.

And they watched over it with whatever they had, while oblivion closed in on them like a mist.

Sometimes Valparaíso twitches like a wounded whale. It flounders in the air, is in agony, dies, and comes back to life.

Every native of the city carries in him the memory of an earthquake. He is a petal of fear clinging all his life to the city's heart. Every native is a hero even before he is born. Because in the memory of the port itself there is defeat, the shudder of the earth as it quakes and the rumble that surfaces from deep down as if a city under the sea, under the land, were tolling the bells in its buried towers to tell man that it's all over.

Sometimes when the walls and the roofs have come crashing down in dust and flames, down into the screams and the silence, when everything seems to have been silenced by death once and for all, there rises out of the sea, like the final apparition, the mountainous wave, the immense green arm that surges, tall and menacing, like a tower of vengeance, to sweep away whatever life remains within its reach.

Sometimes it all begins with a vague stirring, and those who are sleeping wake up. Sleeping fitfully, the soul reaches down to profound roots, to their very depth under the earth. It has always wanted to know it. And knows it now. And then, during the great tremor, there is nowhere to run, because the gods have gone away, the vainglorious churches have been ground up into heaps of rubble.

This is not the terror felt by someone running from a furious bull, a threatening knife, or water that swallows everything. This is a cosmic terror, an instant danger, the universe caving in and crumbling away. And, meanwhile, the earth lets out a muffled sound of thunder, in a voice no one knew it had.

The dust raised by the houses as they came crashing down settles little by little. And we are left alone with our dead, with all the dead, not knowing how we happen to be still alive.

The stairs start out from the bottom and from the top, winding as they climb. They taper off like strands of hair, give you a slight respite, and then go straight up. They become dizzy. Plunge down. Drag out. Turn back. They never end.

How many stairs? How many steps to the stairs? How many feet on the steps? How many centuries of footsteps, of going down and back up with a book, tomatoes, fish, bottles, bread? How many thousands of hours have worn away the steps, making them into little drains where the rain runs down, playing and crying?

Stairways!

No other city has spilled them, shed them like petals into its history, down its own face, fanned them into the air and put them together again, as Valparaíso has. No city has had on its face these furrows where lives come and go, as if they were always going up to heaven or down into the earth.

Stairs that have given birth, in the middle of their climb,

to a thistle with purple flowers! Stairs the sailor, back from Asia, went up only to find a new smile or a terrifying absence in his house! Stairs down which a staggering drunk dived like a black meteor! Stairs the sun climbs to go make love to the hills!

If we walk up and down all of Valparaíso's stairs, we will have made a trip around the world.

Valparaíso of my sorrows . . . ! What happened in the solitudes of the South Pacific? Wandering star or battle of glow-worms whose phosphorescence survived the disaster?

Night in Valparaíso! A speck on the planet lit up, ever so tiny in the empty universe. Fireflies flickered and a golden horseshoe started burning in the mountains.

What happened then is that the immense deserted night set up its formation of colossal figures that seeded light far and wide. Aldebaran trembled, throbbing far above, Cassiopeia hung her dress on heaven's doors, while the noiseless chariot of the Southern Cross rolled over the night sperm of the Milky Way.

Then the rearing, hairy Sagittarius dropped something, a diamond from his hidden hooves, a flea from his hide, very far above.

Valparaíso was born, bright with lights, and humming, edged with foam and meretricious.

Night in its narrow streets filled up with black water nymphs. Doors lurked in the darkness, hands pulled you in, the bedsheets in the south led the sailor astray. Polyanta, Tritetonga, Carmela, Flor de Dios, Multicula, Berenice, Baby Sweet packed the beer taverns, they cared for those who had survived the shipwreck of delirium, relieved one another and were replaced, they danced listlessly, with the melancholy of my rain-haunted people.

The sturdiest whaling vessels left port to subdue leviathan. Other ships sailed for the Californias and their gold. The last of them crossed the Seven Seas later to pick up from the Chilean desert cargoes of the nitrate that lies like the limitless dust of a statue crushed under the driest stretches of land in the world. These were the great adventures.

Valparaíso shimmered across the night of the world. In from the world and out into the world, ships surged, dressed up like fantastic pigeons, sweet-smelling vessels, starved frigates held up overlong by Cape Horn. . . . In many instances, men who had just hit port threw themselves down on the grass. . . . Fierce and fantastic days when the oceans opened into each other only at the far-off Patagonian strait. Times when Valparaíso paid good money to the crews that spit on her and loved her.

A grand piano arrived on some ship; on another, Flora Tristan, Gauguin's Peruvian grandmother, passed through; and on yet another, on the *Wager*, the original Robinson Crusoe came in, in the flesh, recently picked up at the Juan Fernández Islands. . . . Other ships brought pineapples, coffee, black pepper from Sumatra, bananas from Guayaquil, jasmine tea from Assam, anise from Spain. . . . The remote bay, the Centaur's rusty horseshoe, filled with intermittent gusts of fragrance: in one street you were overwhelmed by a sweetness of cinnamon; in another, the smell of custard apples shot right through your being like a white arrow; the detritus of seaweed from all over the Chilean sea came out to challenge you.

Valparaíso then would light up and turn a deep gold; it

was gradually transformed into an orange tree by the sea, it had leaves, it had coolness and shade, it was resplendent with fruit.

The hills of Valparaíso decided to dislodge their inhabitants, to let go of the houses on top, to let them dangle from cliffs that are red with clay, yellow with gold thimble flowers, and a fleeting green with wild vegetation. But houses and people clung to the heights, writhing, digging in, worrying, their hearts set on staying up there, hanging on, tooth and nail, to each cliff. The port is a tug-of-war between the sea and nature, untamed on the cordilleras. But it was man who won the battle little by little. The hills and the sea's abundance gave the city a pattern, making it uniform, not like a barracks, but with the variety of spring, its clashing colors, its resonant bustle. The houses became colors: a blend of amaranth and yellow, crimson and cobalt, green and purple. And Valparaíso carried out its mission as a true port, a great sailing vessel that has run aground but is still alive, a fleet of ships with their flags to the wind. The wind of the Pacific Ocean deserved a city covered with flags.

I have lived among these fragrant, wounded hills. They are abundant hills, where life touches one's heart with numberless shanties, with unfathomable snaking spirals and the twisting loops of a trumpet. Waiting for you at one of these turns are an orange-colored merry-go-round, a friar walking down, a barefoot girl with her face buried in a watermelon, an eddy of sailors and women, a store in a very rusty tin shack, a tiny circus with a tent just large enough for the animal tamer's mustaches, a ladder rising to the clouds, an elevator going up with a full load of onions, seven donkeys carrying water up, a fire truck on the way back from a fire, a store window and in it a collection of bottles containing life or death.

But these hills have profound names. Traveling through these names is a voyage that never ends, because the voyage through Valparaíso ends neither on earth nor in the word. Merry Hill, Butterfly Hill, Polanco's Hill, Hospital, Little Table, Corner, Sea Lion, Hauling Tackle, Potters', Chaparro's, Fern, Litre, Windmill, Almond Grove, Pequenes, Chercanes, Acevedo's, Straw, Prison, Vixens', Doña Elvira's, St. Stephen's, Astorga, Emerald, Almond Tree, Rodríguez's, Artillery, Milkmen's, Immaculate Conception, Cemetery, Thistle, Leafy Tree, English Hospital, Palm Tree, Queen Victoria's, Caravallo's, St. John of God, Pocuro's, Cove, Goat, Biscayne, Don Elias's, Cape, Sugar Cane, Lookout, Parrasia, Quince, Ox, Flower.

I can't go to so many places. Valparaíso needs a new sea monster, an eight-legged one that will manage to cover all of it. I make the most of its immensity, its familiar immensity, but I can't take in all of its multicolored right flank, the green vegetation on its left, its cliffs or its abyss.

I can only follow it through its bells, its undulations, and its names.

Above all, through its names, because they are taproots and rootlets, they are air and oil, they are history and opera; red blood runs in their syllables.

Translated by Hardie St. Martin

Valparaíso, My Love

Osvaldo Rodríguez Musso

WHEN NIGHT FALLS and the sea is the only mirror left to the sky, when the reflection off the waters blends into the first lights, or maybe at dawn when everything is draped in the bluest color of tranquility, then one can see how Valparaíso drops its tears of light over the water.

Early in the morning one can watch the *caballitos mudanceros* (as the Cuban writer, Alejo Carpentier, called them): beasts of burden waiting on street corners to carry up the hills loads as varied as barrels of beer, an immodest bed with wooden legs, maybe a large wardrobe with a solemn mirror, its huge tottering mass sparkling in the morning sun, the mule having disappeared under its weight. They climb up the streets, getting lost as they twist among the wooden structures that hold up the rails of the *ascensores*, which everybody else in the world calls cable cars or funicular railways.

OSVALDO RODRÍGUEZ MUSSO *(1943–96), known popularly as "El Gitano," was born in Valparaíso. He was a musician, visual artist, poet, songwriter, and essayist. One of the most important members of the Chilean New Song Movement, he was exiled in 1973 and spent the remaining years of his life traveling throughout the world. He died in Bardolino, Verona.*

Also in the first hours of the day one can observe the sports fishermen casting their long lines baited with live cuttlefish into the depths and the professional fishermen with their simple panniers, standing facing the sea that still feeds them.

In the houses on high, white garments hung outside to dry blow in the wind; they are handkerchiefs eternally bidding farewell. The houses are made of galvanized tin. As if people knew that rain penetrated everything in Valparaíso, they covered their houses with vertical roofs. Unusual shelters from which the *ascensor* emerges. When that damp, metallic shadow reaches level ground, we enter, and thus begins a slow, noisy ascent that will carry us to the highest miradors from which we can pretend to dominate the indomitable city.

From there we bid farewell to the ships that depart, forever departing. How many ships have weighed anchor in Valparaíso?

We all wanted to be sailors, we all wanted to weigh anchor one day in Valparaíso. We have all walked out on the piers and at one time secretly envied those men who come from far away, from ports that protect one another, that are close to one another, because is there any other port as far away as Valparaíso?

The seagulls fly high, fishing in the sky. The gulls of this port belong to the bravest race of sea birds. They struggle eternally against the wind. Nevertheless, as a child my favorites were always the huge pelicans, friendly, serious birds, waiting reverentially next to the fishing boats for scraps they will catch in the air.

These gigantic pelicans are as tranquil as the large sea

lions that hang around the bay as if they were right at home. We are in a fast rowboat when suddenly a head as large as a horse's, but round and polished with small lively eyes and a clown's moustache, appears. He looks at us, interrogating us: are we fishermen? do we have food for him? No, we are humble oarsmen crossing the bay in a boat pitifully light and fragile. The sea lion feels compassion for our futile efforts, snorts disapprovingly into the surface of the water, soaking us with artificial drizzle, then dives down, oily, barely disturbing the sea's calm surface.

We have all wanted to have a house in the heights of Valparaíso. A tall house through which the wind whistles. Like the one we called The Haunted House when we were kids, an old mansion surrounded by high walls for which our adolescent imaginations invented strange lights that roamed around at night through darkened rooms. Or those houses that look like wood-framed castles in the area around the headquarters of the Maipo Regiment near the San Pedro Gardens. Houses with corridors, hallways, balustrades, balconies decorated with silent gargoyles and miniature caryatids, all carved in Douglas fir. Houses that vibrate with the south winds of summer and the north winds of winter. Houses that vibrate like boats in a storm, crying, moaning under the watery onslaught, then singing in summer when the sun exposes all their secrets.

There are houses that appear to have rejected windows but have nonetheless retained the solemnity of a high look-out tower, like houses in Tuscany that seem to rise out of their battlements. But in Valparaíso, they are always wood-framed and from them will peer children who will also want to be sailors.

And the man who created this architecture, he who struggled to bring with him the old European style, adorned his lintels with flowers and garlands made of fake stones, imitation baroque, neoclassical, and renaissance sculptures until the earthquakes come and leave their permanent and cyclopean imprint.

In front of some of these old houses a few unlit lanterns still hang. How many years have the lanterns of Valparaíso stood without light? After the boom and the abandon came technology; notable men came and went, those who loved Valparaíso and those who didn't. The avenues filled up with tall, modern, square lamps utterly lacking in charm, but a few old streetlights still hang in their blind permanence from some corners. They are petrified seagulls, frozen in their solitude.

Thus grew this port; nobody knows whether it is the last one of the north or the first one of the south. Nobody knows because in summer, when the south wind comes with its invisible broom and sweeps all the clouds from the bluest of skies, it is dry and parched. That is when Valparaíso fades in the heat and our eyes are assaulted with incessant flashes and violent contrasts of light and shadow. In the winter it grows dark, the north wind intervenes, steals our hats, soaks us with interminable rains, releases the gale winds that whistle through the tin siding and set the electric wires trembling.

The Dutch documentary filmmaker Jorge Ivens said that the four elemental symbols of Valparaíso are the wind, stairways, fire, and blood. To these one must add others from much different but no less important categories of things, such as the miniature gardens that grow in the wood planters in most of Valparaíso's humble windows. These gardens are not planted along the shaded boulevards lined with palm trees and antique bronze statues, but rather grow in the hills, and their principal flower is ostentatiously called *cardenal* even though the rest of the world calls them geraniums. And the *ascensores*, those that have been abandoned and have died from inactivity like the great lanterns and have been overgrown with moss and ivy. And the tombstones in the cemeteries, many of which tell us stories about loneliness in other languages . Also, the blue stones that pave some of the roads leading up to the hills and that came from England as ballast in the sailboats.

And the sea, definitely the sea.

Where else could there be a port in which the ships must leave the bay and lay to in a storm? Throughout history, many couldn't manage and ended smashed against the rocks along the coast. This is an authentic anti-port even though its name means Valley of Paradise. Perhaps, on that mysterious day when Juan de Saavedra approached its beaches, the wind went into hiding for a few hours to allow the Spanish captain the rare spectacle of a calm bay worthy of that name. This sometimes happens right in the middle of summer, but only briefly and at an unpredictable time.

All night I hear the raging storm that shakes the windows, whistles through the vines in the garden, and vibrates along the length of electric lines. It strikes against far-off, unknown doors. The storm and its ghosts are invading the night. From afar blows a boat's siren asking for help. The day delays its dawning and I am fifteen years old.

I wait impatiently for the morning so that I can go and

look the storm in the eye. The first glance out my window shows me a world destroyed. The hills have been erased, the horizon is so close I can touch it. The bay is emptied of boats; I see only a lifeboat, like a legend, crossing the rough inlet on the other side of the breakwater, Molo de Abrigo. The sea is the dirty color of *café con leche* because the rain has once again stolen the sand from the hills, carrying it through the veins of the river beds, and dyeing the sea for as far as the eye can see. The rest is submerged in a low, tenebrous fog.

Huge waves are crashing over the highest point of the breakwater. The fishing schooners that are anchored together for protection are being tossed about like matchboxes in an avalanche. I observe as three black flags—to indicate the approach of what they call a level three storm—are raised over Silva Palma Fort. I run to my girlfriend's house; now is the time to go to the beach.

South of Valparaíso, at the end of Altamirano Avenue and before the Piedra Feliz Wall is Playa de las Torpederas, or Beach of the Torpedo Boats. Strange name. A riddle? It is said that it got its name because it was used to shelter the launches that were supposed to protect the bay from a possible attack during World War II. Though it is too exposed to the north winds and offers no protection during the winter, just like the rest of the coves of the port, it is an excellent observation spot from which to look the storm right in the face.

The infuriated sea gathers its strength, its anger rising into an enormous wave that appears spontaneously behind the fog. We scream and run up to the cement barrier. Then we hear the dull sound of the rocks being dragged out by the undertow; the wind blows everything to bits; the birds have escaped.

Soon the mass of water will come to drown us, to punish our impudence. We run to escape it. In vain. The enormous wave crashes with a deafening roar, like the blast of a cannon, it rises eight, ten meters high, is pulverized in the wind, reaches the other side of the promenade, to the foot of the hill, and soaks us from head to toe.

This is the winter game of those who are young and in love and in Valparaíso.

Translated by Katherine Silver

Seaside Resort
Adolfo Couve

I

CARTAGENA, THE SEASIDE RESORT, that dirty beach, abandoned every winter, that stage set, that façade, that infinite decrepitude; pointed roofs, eaves full of bats, windows without shutters opening onto the sea that lives in them as it does the nooks between the rocks. Decaying balconies, service stairways, locked up and rotted away, weather vanes, rusted and frozen, iron birds that stand up obstinately to the persistent winds. Drizzle that sends the hungry gulls away from the waves, organized gangs of coots that engrave their hurried steps in the black sand, and signs along the crooked streets whose spelling mistakes squeak and sway.

Beyond the sea wall, the ocean lifts a fan of foam from its depths; it breaks apart and throws itself against the broken balustrades. The dogs are afraid of this deep roar, the

---

ADOLFO COUVE *(1940–98) was born in Valparaíso. He studied art in Chile, Paris, and New York. Although he gained considerable fame as a painter, his greatest achievements are thought to be his literary works, which include ten volumes of novels, novellas, and short stories. He committed suicide in his mansion in Cartagena in 1998.*

---

sound of water laboring ceaselessly, taking centuries to change a shape; a roar that also rises to the houses that hang from the cliffs, their original colors now faded, their enormous open rooms rendered uninhabitable, the floorboards buckling under the tread of restless souls.

Like a familiar backdrop once again hung in place this summer: the blue of the sea and the sky.

The bustle of the crowds, the brightly colored striped canvases that spread their sparkling shade, the shouts of the bullhorn, and the breeze all run parallel to the trampled sand, dark, turned upside down.

Up above, on top of the sea wall, next to the banister, a woman, well advanced in years, takes refuge under a parasol that submerges her in her own ambiance, softening the edges, the deep contrasts of her face. She partakes of summer only by showing a pair of skinny bare arms from which the skin hangs as if detached. The complex weave of her lace gloves protects her hands. She holds tightly onto the handle of her parasol shaped like the head of a dragon with green scales, its lively eyes unperturbed by the day's glare.

Her dress, a summery shift, has traveled in her suitcase many seasons. The belt with a fancy buckle doesn't match. Hanging from her arm is the only leather purse in sight. Her legs end in polished white shoes, also unfashionable.

But her attitude—there among those men dripping water, children carrying buckets and shovels, women whose extra flesh jiggles outside the scanty straps of their bathing suits—seems to be a refusal to capitulate to her condition as an old woman, and she awaits a miracle, because she says to herself, "If I am alive, it is impossible that nothing will happen to me." And the sea answers her by pulling itself up, sonorous and harsh in its fluctuations, only to return with a gigantic and transparent outburst of laughter.

Angelica Bow doesn't flinch. She has faced worse adversaries than the lack of opportunity, and her large eyes, heavily made up and framed by blush and false eyelashes, impudently watch the young men, their wide-backed torsos, athletic arms and necks, playful heads full of sand, mussed by the wind.

She cannot even go down to the beach, not because she is afraid of being knocked over by the swimmers, but because she is worried about getting her high heels stuck in the dunes. She is a lady: she wears a scarf to protect her coiffed hair from the wind and is surrounded by a different light, more subdued and tenuous than the inhospitable and blinding glare the sun spreads over the others.

She slowly makes her way to the car that awaits her amid makeshift kiosks and garbage. Araneda, her chauffeur, respectfully opens the back door. Angelica closes her parasol and lets the dragon sleep with open eyes on the seat beside her.

Tomorrow, at the same time of day, she will return for her walk along the promenade in front of the waves when the setting sun, almost transparent, and its clamor muffle even the bullhorn that announces lost children and the aimless wanderings of the seagulls that can only fly and caw flush with the sea foam and the crowds.

II

Her summer house in Cartagena is so huge that an entire wing remains under lock and key. Built into the cliff, it turns its back on the horizon and has a front garden that ends in a fence bordering the abyss. There, as nowhere else, bloom roses, succulents, many-colored hibiscus, *cochabam-binas*, and camellias.

With decisive snips of the pruning shears, Angelica cuts two roses every afternoon to perfume her bedroom; facing its pure blue picture window stands an armoire of uncertain style with three sections, whose mirrors reflect water, tides, and the undertow. Next to the curtains rests a dressing table with tapered legs, its surface littered with a disordered array of jars of cream and boxes of powders.

The double bed stands in the middle of the room, and one can clearly see the place where Angelica lays down her body. The indentation shows that she has been a widow for many years, that she does not share that draped space with anyone.

The frayed branches and flowerpots of the worn rug, like an unwatered garden, show the passage of time. The exposed weave tells of the many steps endured, the asperity, the routine, a life's footprints.

III

With great force, she turns the key in the lock, then unbuttons her dress, removes her shoes, and lies down on the bed. A teardrop slips into a deep furrow that traverses her face, then runs down to moisten the pillow. Her lips are parted, there is a novel on the bedside table, and her veined hand mechanically turns the knobs on the portable radio. Soon, a deep masculine voice sings her the season's hit song, speaking to her with adoration, telling her that she will forever be his most dearly beloved, a keening saxophone corroborates the singer's seductions, and her clear sky clouds over, and the plaster vase with embossed palm trees and pompons seems to tremble in the breeze that sweeps along the coastline outside the window.

> *Now I will adore you as I've never done before;*
> *because I am and will forever be*
> *the one who loves you best,*

and the sax again calls to her as her modest slip and embroidered corset rise and fall over her pounding heart.

Then she gets up and faces the water-filled mirror on the armoire and daringly lowers the straps of her slip; now, naked to the waist, she caresses her flaccid breasts, her wrinkled belly, her ancient disproportionate shapes. And as she lifts her breasts, she lets the slip fall to her feet. There she stands, naked, barely protected by the delicate panty she is unable to remove.

A body devastated as if by a careless sculptor, and behind, the radiance of the ocean and the sky, the immensity that outlines the thin legs and dyed hair. A few timid knocks on the door bring her back; it is Bernarda announcing that tea has been served. She can barely answer, the room inundated by that popular song that repeats insistently:

> *Don't even try to find another love like mine,*
> *because I am and will forever be*
> *the one who loves you best.*

IV

When she arrives at the beach, and after she gets out of the car, she orders the chauffeur to return to the house. His presence disturbs her.

"Araneda, leave me here alone, go back and clean the ter-

race, sweep the garden, then come get me at tea time . . .
not before five o'clock."

And while the car makes it way back up the winding
road, she opens her parasol, tightly grips the scaly dragon,
and begins her aimless stroll in front of the blinding brilliance that slides toward her from the horizon, filtered
through the waves, attenuating, with its intensity, the pro-
fusion of colors in the sand.

She cannot find a place to sit down: the benches are full
of vacationers. She walks slowly toward the flea market, El
Persa, her shadow following her like a dog. The texture of
her lace gloves pressed against the dragon feels like teeth.
And if the breeze gets any stronger, it can tease out a pair
of teardrops that always hover in the corners of those atten-
tive, overly made-up eyes, eyes that are horrified as they
confirm her current reality, her complete lack of participa-
tion in the world swirling so closely around her.

Sometimes the people sitting on the benches notice her,
but generally nobody apprehends the full contrast between
those agile, naked bodies and this languid pedestrian,
dressed in white, under an equally lonely and anachronistic
parasol.

The violet patch of her shadow follows her but seems also
to hide from her, and after Araneda parks to pick her up, it
vanishes, relieved, as soon as the old woman gets into the car.

The noisy nights of the seaside resort keep her awake,
and flashes of light pierce the moon in the mirror, furtively
illuminating the plaster leaves that decorate the unlit lamp.

She reviews the day, pondering that episode with the
leaky faucet in the bathroom sink that morning, remembering the young man who came to fix it, the penetrating scent
of sweat, and his insinuations as he turned the wrench.

"I can do anything for you, señora . . . if you know what I mean. All I ask for is a new shirt, or whatever you want to give me. . . ."

Angelica, standing in the doorframe, pretended not to hear his suggestions, because she considered them improper, but later, during her daily search in front of the breakwater, they came back to her. What had stopped her? The suddenness of the situation? Shame at exposing the decadence of her body? Fear of being at the mercy of a strapping young man whose name she didn't even know?

There, lying on her back, watching the lights that shine intermittently on the mirror and the ceiling and then depart, she regrets her reserve. How she would have loved to have an affair, an illusion during this, perhaps her last, summer. Sit down at the table where her friends her age deal out their hours playing cards, and when they scold her for being distracted, break into a complicitous smile that nobody would imagine was provoked by her falling into the arms of a muscular plumber who had impregnated her impeccably clean sheets and pillows with his sour odor, the same that hovered so long in the bathroom.

"Angelica, what are you thinking about. Don't you feel well? Pick, pick, it's your turn, here's the deck. I'm out with an eight card canasta, and not a single wild card."

And below, Araneda, standing in front of the Chevrolet, reading the afternoon paper. "How terrible would it have been if, when I get home after visiting my friends, I see the plumber leaning against the gate, waiting for me, or if he called me in the middle of the night. Men like that, all they want is money, nothing else, and then one day I would wake up dead in my bed. A shirt, that's how it begins. . . . That's why I prefer the promenade, there I don't know anybody, and now that I send Araneda home, just maybe, one of these afternoons, some charming swimmer will offer to take me to one of those hotels on the main beach."

"How're you doing? What's your name?"

"Cartagena. And you?"

"Darling, people like me don't have names. Or didn't you know that? Are you alone?"

"Yes."

And Angelica smiles tonight at these dialogues. The dragon with hard green scales, his eyes open, wide awake, insomniac like his owner, seems to guess her thoughts, because he stares at her from the dresser in the shadows.

v

What if I go out at night? At night all cats look black, as they say, and she ties a spotted scarf over her hair.

"Bernarda, tell Araneda to get the Chevrolet ready. I'm going out."

The maid, her mouth gaping in astonishment, doesn't dare argue with the widow and does as she is told.

The dragon on the parasol watches as Angelica dresses in front of the darkened mirror, and its glass eyes look sadly at that identical dragon also left alone on a dresser.

The car descends along the winding road and rolls slowly toward the crowd so tightly packed that it barely moves along the promenade toward the Hotel Bahia. That whole mass under colored lights against a dark, nonexistent ocean.

Around the corner are the games: the ferris wheel, its lights going round and round, mirrored below where the water rumbles; and the roller coaster, the screaming riders enclosed in the canvas-topped caterpillar that rises and falls disjointedly.

Angelica joins the crowd. But she only gets as far as the game with the ducks that get knocked down only to reappear automatically like the chorus in an operetta. And the pile of stuffed cats falls to the ground when the roulette wheel slowly recovers its colors and numbers as the rubber stopper catches on the nail.

Someone wins a sleeping doll, a can of peaches, an old bottle of champagne.

Angelica would be happy to settle in among the bottles in the next game and wait for some young man to throw a wooden ring around her neck. Imagining herself imprisoned in that narrow space with the crowd about to undress her, she is surprised by a cotton candy vendor offering her a blushing late-afternoon cloud.

Further on, the caramel apples, the old magazines, the merry-go-round of gentle Dumbos that prance along, their backs pierced by bronze bars.

After an hour of pushing against the crowd, her hair a mess, she manages to find her chauffeur, who comes to her rescue.

She prefers to drive around on the other side of the ferris wheel, watching from inside the car as clouds of sugar and caramel apples descend like setting suns into the sea of people.

Cartagena, the seaside resort, that dirty beach, abandoned every winter, that stage set, that façade, that infinite decrepitude, pointed roofs, lost in the crowd like wreckage adrift.

Translated by Katherine Silver

Isla Negra

Marjorie Agosín

THE SWEET NIGHTTIME HOURS are like a thick forest. After so many years of clinging to the same dream,
words spoken in strange languages fold and unfold, confused like hollow sunflowers at night. You ask me to tell
you about my time on the islands, to whisper in your ear
about the beat of your heart next to mine, like the most
hidden, sleepy forest.

I will tell you about Isla Negra, about those summers
when the days marched by, openly, perpetually, like the
movements of water and light. I was wearing white because
I was fifteen years old and my mother decided it was advis-
able to play with transparency. Then I went down to the
beach where at times I saw Pablo Neruda, sitting motionless for hours, persevering half asleep by the great ocean.

His voice was also like that of the ocean, fraught with

MARJORIE AGOSÍN *(1955–) is an award-winning poet,
short-story writer, and human rights activist. Her most recent volumes
of poetry are* Dear Anne Frank, An Absence of Shadows, *and*
Desert Rain. *She is currently professor and chair of the Spanish
department at Wellesley College. She lives in Massachusetts with her
husband and two children.*

shadows and clarity. I knelt and slid my hands along the sand, sensing the moss of the steep rocks, the immensity of time hollowed above the starfish. I immersed myself in profound joy because that was life, and happiness was there, resting a moment in a watery garden.

The island meant contemplation of time outside of time, a mute heart gazing upon the bliss of nature unfolding. It was a world without a compass, a world attached to the storm of things, and I sensed the glory of being alive.

I tell you all this here, on the other side of America, where you do not know this tale, a talisman of memories, a precious crown. But this, too, is your story. It will live here, on this night of dreams, upon backs that turn like wheels. You tell me a story, and I will tell you one. It thrills me to tell you that I, too, love you, far from the islands, on the closeness of your skin.

I would see him, walking majestically. Sometimes he seemed to disappear from the world, then return to look at it once more. I liked to watch him, to pause over the most trivial detail of his beauty: small snails, beyond sound and human time, seaweed like the hair of luxuriant women. His gait and sense of wonder were slow, and no matter the season he wore an enormous Araucan poncho. At dawn, when the beach like a solitary woman recovers its spectacular beauty, he sat on the craggy rock, rolled up his shirtsleeves, hoping to capture the ocean's breath and stars, unfettered and free. He began to write, pressing against his knees, as if affirming his existence between the sky and the sea. His hands dreamed dizzily of cities inhabited by poetry. He seemed alone, yet full of love. That is how I saw him when I was a child. I saw and heard the women of the village say, "There goes Don Pablo." They did not call him Poet Neruda.

I liked to see him with his notebooks, pages dense with green ink, like moss and the peace of victory. I wanted to be a poet, too, and I learned to love things that unhinged and resembled absence.

For a long time, I saw Pablo Neruda walk along the coast of Isla Negra, and his presence inspired me to write.

In September the autumn breezes throbbed, and that great silence of sprites, fairies, and bitter dust could be felt up and down the avenues. Back then the streets and houses were empty. It was a time outside of time. The dictators cleaned the shiny streets with the faces of the embalmed dead. Then, on September 23, rumors spread of the poet's burial. Everyone knew who he was. He was nameless because his name belonged to all, as did his poems and words flowing from him like the fluid movement of the seasons.

Suddenly a slow cortège passed by, like the march of death, like the sighs of memory. They arrived with the sun, with wounded butterflies. Those empty avenues began to fill with the murmur of footsteps and breathing, a small seedbed of memories. All the laundresses came out with their white handkerchiefs, the young girls with their star-drawing pencils, the sad men, the widows, and the orphans.

Poetry was overwhelmed by the footsteps making their way through the throng of mourners. Their tongues gave more than life. Alongside the cortège, poetry also spoke. The poet's language became many languages. His widow looked skyward. She raised her arms, not pleading, but in victory. From the stilled voice in the casket came many voices of lovers who had hidden beyond the avenues, of secret, clandestine love affairs.

In my country, when they buried the poet, the land became a carpet of flowers. Among the tears were smiles, and for an instant, the night of the dictator gave way to the day's victory. A man had died, but not his words. Pablo Neruda had died in his house by the sea.

When we left our country during the military dictatorship, I lost my own face for years. There were no grottos in Georgia, and my head sank into my pillow, into the red earth. Soldiers surrounded Neruda's stone house, but the faithful, with their passion for life, inscribed its gate with poems and placed small, enchanted wildflowers in front of it. The house became like a sleepwalker. It was alone, but the words lodging in it are immutable. Years later, when the tyrants in heavy, thrashing boots fell from power, the house was opened. We returned to Chile with courage and dignity, and were able to go inside. Like mischievous children we played with the model trains that light up the surrounding landscape. Respectfully, we picked up the poet's secret belongings and put them away, our joy flowing through the windows toward the Pacific Ocean. The bells, fraught with the smell of ocean breezes, shaped like waterfalls and waves, were still there. They were the reason why I wanted to return, to keep the memory, to recover my mother's tiny stones, to pick blazing *aromo* flowers that are like robust tangles of sunlight.

Today I return to the Chilean coast with my grand-

mother, who is almost ninety, and my young son. I tell them
to press their faces against the rocks that taste of secret
grottos, that are as tall as the stars and the treetops, and they
do as I ask. I lean against them. At last I have returned
home. I trusted in words and poetry, and the country is once
again decked out in its very best clothes.

Translated by Nancy Abraham Hall

–{ Heartland }–

Until She Go No More
Beatriz García-Huidobro

IN THE SPRING the country elects a new president. For
months beforehand, the candidates and those who wish
to rise with the winner visit towns and hold large fiestas in
the plazas, the city halls, and the community centers. Big
trucks drive through the outlying villages and farms and
invite people to come with them to San Juan. Huge
crowds gather; the houses are all decked out with garlands
and flags; they set up loudspeakers and microphones; or-
chestras play; photographers pursue their subjects relent-
lessly. Representatives of the different political parties
pass out wine in exchange for votes. They fill up buckets

BEATRIZ GARCÍA-HUIDOBRO *(1959–) was born in
Santiago. She writes textbooks, novels for children and young adults,
and recently published her second novel,* Sombras nada más. *This text
is taken from her first novel,* Until She Go No More. *It is the story of
a nameless, motherless peasant girl told through her own voice. This sec-
tion describes the advent of the socialist movement that led to the election of Salvador Allende in 1970. The geographic names in the text are
invented, but the area portrayed is in Chile's VII Region. This novel
was a finalist for the Sor Juana Inés de la Cruz Prize in Mexico.*

99

with punch and serve it with large ladles to avid recipients who hold out their cups while mumbling unintelligible sentences pregnant with obsequiousness.

People leave in droves from hamlets like ours and reach the valley only after walking for three exhausting days. They go, in spite of the cold, the hostility of the rocky, uneven roads, the temporary abandon in which they leave their lands, and without a thought about sleeping under nothing but a coat of stars and a cold blanket of dew.

Finally, the trucks leave the vacant lots where they were parked and the ingratiating smiles grow distant.

Night falls and its blackness howls.

The return trip is long. Everyone is gorged on promises. They may never vote or may not be even functionally literate. The man who was patted on the back by a candidate is already a new man. Wiser. Different. A fundamental part of the incommensurable. As if that hand, through some kind of osmosis, had rendered him transcendent, covered him with a layer of worldliness.

"It's all a big lie," Aunt Berta concludes.

I want to go to San Juan. During the election six years ago, my father didn't want to go to any candidate's rally. That year, the only man he respected had withdrawn from the race. Now he is up for reelection. He is a gentleman with white hair and eyes that are clear and transparent. My father wants to see him and hear his words. When they announce his arrival, we will all go to the valley. My brothers are already registered and must listen as adults to the voice of the man they will vote for.

The east wind begins to lick the ground. A few leaves

lend a red tint to the landscape. The sky is streaked with white shreds. Amelia is bent over, doing the wash. . . .

The song is joyous and melodious.

As she approaches, we recognize her voice.

Ester has arrived.

Pedro lives with Rosita now that she is pregnant. At first, he wants to bring her here, but doña Herminia needs a man to work her uncultivated fields. Amelia wants another woman in the house. My father cannot spare two sets of hands. Aunt Berta says that my brother is not obliged to marry Rosita. That if he does so to make up for the damage, Rosita should be grateful and not steal from my father like that, because the sons he has raised are his assets. Doña Herminia argues that her land will belong to the husband of her daughter and their children. That Pedro should begin to work the inheritance of his descendants.

My father finally gives in. The cock's crow at dawn turns into the pitch darkness that precedes the sunrise and the restfulness of the afternoon into night's heavy fatigue.

Amelia doesn't speak. She angrily throws the grain to the hungry chickens. I tell her it is better this way. Rosita is a woman, and we should support a decision that favors women. She says only:

"They wouldn't have made a fool of me so easily."

Her gesture is arrogant and her voice is sharp. She walks proudly toward the house with a sure step. Her hands hang trembling by her sides.

Men born in arid lands where germination is slow and flowering rare are not ready for change. The cycle of life must spin slowly and gently wear away the outer layers of bark.

My father shuts Ester up. Her smile no longer pleases him. It is no longer the fresh breeze that he had longed for but rather a gale that batters.

My sister has not come alone. A young man is with her. He is dressed like a peasant, but one can tell from every thread and stitch of his clothes that distant hands have woven the cloth and sewn them. His hair is long, and he has a thick mustache that does not completely cover his frequent and generous smile. Speeches gush out of him, and every word he utters offers a glimpse of the passion contained within his gaunt chest.

People crowd around him and listen but keep their eyes down. Ester lifts her eyes to him. She is quiet. She turns away from him only when something he says elates her and unknown feelings are released within her. His chest vibrates as he speaks and his mouth forms, with each syllable, a secret invitation. Nevertheless, the men do not perceive any threat, the women do not distrust his opulence, the girls don't pay attention to his silky, smooth skin. His words have grown too strong.

Don Victor has a son. His wife died in childbirth. They say that he resented that tiny piece of life that had the power to destroy the other life. While the child was still in his cradle, he left it and went away. Rumor has it that he went to the valley and used the black arts to amass a small fortune. He returned every summer. He dedicated himself to improving the land; he brought machinery and seeds. Shut up in his house, he observed his son's progress. Manuel was thin and dark, the opposite of his father. He was raised to be weak and apprehensive, mirroring the fears of his Aunt Ema, who now depended on the child's survival to maintain the high social standing she had achieved.

Later, don Victor bought half a block in Pedregal and opened the village's first store, with four sections of different kinds of merchandise and a cash register. People hung around outside the door of the shop just to hear the register ring when it opened and closed. He placed his sister Ema in charge and took his son to the valley. Blood mixes differently among members of the same family, and doña Ema turned out to have no talent for business. The shop was taken over by someone sent in by don Victor, and his sister drowned herself in drink. They say the pain of losing the child is what destroyed her. Especially when they sent him to a boarding school in Santiago and she had no way of communicating with him.

Aunt Berta says that Ema was always a lost woman, that she never got married because she had no mysteries left to unveil to a man, that the abyss of alcoholism was a pale reflection of the punishment that awaited her in the afterlife, and that she deserved having the child taken from her as punishment for those poor creatures she tore out of her own belly.

Nobody knows why don Victor returned. His return was gradual and silent as if the earth had displayed its charms and suggestively penetrated his dreams.

Winter departs. The earth changes colors and the first fissures open. The little boy runs to the hillock that overlooks the path. He stands there for hours in the wind, staring at the empty, dusty track.

This is the only image of him Amelia remembers.

"He was waiting for his old man," Ester says.

Pablo says that in the cities men are joining together, that a new movement has awoken the people. That this year centuries of oppression will be brought to an end with a new social order of renovation. He pulls out of his suitcase a machine we've never seen. It plays a tape that overflows with the indomitable song of men and women who will be free. So strong is its message that the night is set on fire and heads are raised with a new vehemence. Pupils shine, lit up by the reflection of what is now carried in the air. Slowly, hesitant mouths begin to sing along. A few days later, those once dull voices have more vigor than the chorus on the tape.

My father prohibits the music and the words on his land. His voice becomes narrower during his solitary vigils. I remain with him. Each time I tell Amelia which pasture the young people will meet in. She says that she is not going to go against her father's will. That my brothers have been poisoned by Pablo and Ester's lies and have run off to listen to them.

Aunt Berta approaches when the moon is high. She tells us where they are and what they have said. Shut up, my father tells her. As if by not speaking, one can weaken the facts. She was not born to be silent and explains the dangers invoked by trying to change the natural order.

Ester tells me that luxuries are not important and that privileges are going to disappear. That the rich will soon be rejected rather than envied. Once everyone has been won over to this way of thinking, jewelry and other fancy things will no longer be made because they only corrupt people by making them want to possess them.

She confesses that she has had some difficulty ridding herself of all vanity but that the *compañeros* in this struggle won't have anything to do with women who wear makeup and jewelry. Without all that, men can see a woman in her full humanity and not through stereotypes and masks. In the end, men and women will walk hand in hand, women will no longer follow behind. The elimination of the oppressed classes will extend to families, schools, factories, and fields.

My father is right. Ester has changed. A handful of repeated words has achieved what the crushing environment of her childhood alone never managed.

Ester leaves one morning. She carries the few things she brought with her. Pablo carries his things and the tape recorder. Everybody is working in the fields at that time of day, but a growing number of men and woman accompany them to the bend in the road. At first it is a slow, silent procession. Soon, a gentle voice begins singing that song that has sunk deeply into their hearts and now rises from all their throats. The tone is impetuous. Winged and silent are the people's steps as they follow around many bends in the uneven road. Only at the crossing does Pablo take leave of them. He reminds them of their commitment to organize and tells them that they are now part of this great undertaking. He urges them to make a great effort, not to be afraid of joining groups from neighboring villages who are also organizing themselves. He and Ester will return soon, he says, and they place their trust in the people, in what they will achieve in the coming weeks.

"Now!" he insists. This is the word most often repeated. It enters my bloodstream and courses through my entire body. I couldn't explain what it means. The now is already here, beating within each of us. I don't know what the now is for others. Or for me.

Some nights, the moon gets into bed with me and throws the covers onto the floor. It slithers up to my eyes and draws back my eyelids. The night is clear, and I see my mother's silhouette. She's bending over, she gets up, she moves her hands diligently in incessant activity. She doesn't move from where she is, as if she can fit only in that one spot on earth.

I can't see her face. I cover my eyes with my hands and arms, trembling. I don't stop pressing them against my face until day breaks.

A fine rain falls. It sticks to the dust covering our clothes then drips down. My father's muddy footsteps are slow and quiet. All around us stir autumn winds with their first sharp pricks of cold.

My sister is going to register to vote. There is no office in the village, just a registrar who comes and works out of don Victor's shop. He sits on a high stool and opens up a large binder. Amelia signs slowly, her face almost touching the page. The man watches her and drums his fingers on the wood. Others wait in line. He looks them up and down scornfully. Amelia is blushing fiercely, and even though her hair is pulled back, some locks fall over her forehead. My father turns his hat slowly in his hands. Time seems to stand still. I pull a few coins out of my pocket and they fall to the ground. They roll away slowly, tracing endless curved paths. Amelia is glued to the pen, and the coins roll; they do not stop rolling.

This is what they say. Not to me. These are commentaries that other voices pick up, send off, and raise again. No hand has been absent from this tangle.

Manuel has arrived in Pedregal accompanied by two young men. They are just like Pablo. They pour words out with the same charm, but they don't do it under the stars nor do they hide away in the hills. They perch themselves on the highest peaks and speak with the light shining on their faces. They walk through the fields and call to men and women. They do not beg. They lead the meetings with a combination of such tenderness and authority that timid sprouts emerge impetuously. Thick roots dig into the earth of breasts and bellies. A blanket of boughs grows with urgency and an open flower blooms from every furrow. A movable forest that unites, intertwines, entangles, and weaves the invisible net of hope.

From all four directions it is being said that don Victor will not welcome Manuel in his house. That Manuel has not knocked on that closed door but has crossed other dusty thresholds. That other doors swing open upon his approach. That places at many tables wait for him. That from every batch there remains for him the whitest bread, the finest offering, the simplest.

On the land that will one day be Pedro's, a small wooden shack is erected in a few days. There people converge in the afternoon to release their weariness, to leave room for the fatigue of forging a new path.

Doña Herminia carries out her business next to the window. She says nothing until the rain starts to fall and women, soaked to the bone, trudge through her fields. Then, she releases the song of their bellies and they race off into the hills. She spends several hours every afternoon in the shack, then she comes and goes, diligently covering many roads washed out by the mud and thus reaching more women. She fills her hands as she empties the women one by one.

We won't be going to San Juan. My father's candidate won't be making an appearance in these parts. But the other one is coming. Ester arrives. Little effort is needed to form a large caravan. They leave happily, and the air grows heavy. The vault of the sky turns gray and narrow, enclosing us in this empty mountainous land.

My brothers leave. Rosa and the child, just a few days old, remain with us. My father has grown old. The furrows no longer fit in his skin and grow deeper and wider each day. His body withers; he is but one more crevice filled with seed that does not sprout.

Rain hangs in the cracks. The walls are damp. I push against them with my face, my back, my sides. My clothes get wet, and through my skin I absorb the water, swelling within me that which I can no longer contain, even though I don't know what it is or how to let it out.

Don Victor tells me that they are going to elect that idiot. That he has promised the impossible. And that when the party is over and the morning after brings hangovers and disappointment, he won't be the one to listen to them moaning and complaining about their fallow fields. That the valleys are not going to be parceled out and given to insignificant peasants. They will dispossess one oligarchy only to create a new one, a new power that has no history.

I don't understand his words. Nor those of the others. But don Victor's are hard and bitter, they strike out, they cloud the vision, while the others dig into the earth and bring forth flowers that carry within them the gentle thrust of the wind.

Translated by Katherine Silver

The Ghost of the German Voyeur

Patricio Riveros Olavarría

I

"AROUND HERE, it's not so unusual for the dead to walk around at night," says Justino Mamani. "Every evening, right after the sun slips behind the mountain, it's the same old thing, seeing them wandering from here to there and from there to here, as if they thought San Lorenzo de Tarapaca belonged to them. But you've got to keep your eyes peeled 'cause it's easy to bump into them; they're just like a patch of fog, like clouds you've always thought were made of cotton and then an airplane flies right through them. Anyway, it's not a good idea to cross paths with these beings from the other world, because each time you do, they steal a little piece of your soul. Of course the ones

PATRICIO RIVEROS OLAVARRÍA *(1962–) was born in Iquique and lived for many years in Holland and Cuba. He has received numerous literary prizes in Cuba, Chile, and Spain, and has written hundreds of stories, novellas, and one novel. He currently resides in Iquique, where he directs his own radio and television shows and continues to work in print journalism.*

out wandering around are the ones who can't rest. That's why I try to be good—I don't want to give the living a hard time after I die. And I try to help those miserable creatures so they can return to their sacred stomping grounds and rest in eternal peace."

The few streets of this dusty town in the middle of the Tarapaca desert have been drying out for centuries in a sun that hasn't known a moment's rest for all that time; just as the pounding hooves of horses and the mill's grinding stone turn wheat into flour, the fire of the sun has turned this soil into talc. The dust is so fine that the silent steps of insects leave traces. And in the mornings one can easily spot marks left by the ghosts during their nocturnal strolls.

Don Justino has devoted his life to helping these poor souls find peace, taking advantage of the religious festival honoring the patron saint of San Lorenzo to help him do so; and thanks to him, very few still wander aimlessly through the streets of San Lorenzo de Tarapaca.

"Not like in Iquique," asserts don Justino, "where there are so many dead roaming the streets at night and stealing little pieces of souls that the population is being left soulless. Obviously, ghosts in the city are more discreet, and they don't hang out in Prat Plaza or Balmaceda Park; they haunt dark alleyways, and when they run across someone who's stoned or drunk, they grab them. The people in Iquique have no idea what's going on. A few months ago I tried to open their eyes, to warn them that their Free Trade Zone and their modern apartment buildings that reach up to the sky are all being left without souls. I spoke about it on several radio stations and wrote about it in the local newspapers, and all they said was that I needed to see a psychiatrist. They don't want to know why so many people's eyes are dull, why so many individuals think only about themselves, why so many wander around like zombies. Drug addicts are the first to lose their souls because they sleep all day and get up at the same time as the soul snatchers. Sometimes I think drug addicts get up just so they can offer their souls to the highest bidder. Well, what can I do? Even if they took me seriously, there'd be nothing I could do in Iquique. There are too many wandering, sinful dead for a wasted, dried-up old man like me to deal with."

11

The religious festival for the patron saint of San Lorenzo de Tarapaca is much smaller than the one for the Virgin of Carmen in La Tirana, so there are fewer religious dances, fewer believers, fewer observers, fewer beautiful multicolored costumes, fewer brass instruments, drums, and flutes, fewer penitents dragging themselves along the ground, fewer people selling drinks and fried foods, fewer merchants selling countless different images of the saint, fewer good-bye tears, fewer vows, and fewer petitions. Nevertheless, the setting of the town itself is much more picturesque. The houses of San Lorenzo, made of mud and stone, are nestled in a narrow valley about a mile wide bordered on both sides by two parallel barren ridges roughly two to three hundred yards high to the east and to the west; the valley boasts greenery so sparse that only in the desert would it appear lush and hopeful. There the sun disappears early: by 5:30 in the afternoon, a cool shadow is already draping itself gently over the town.

The church tower, about sixty feet high and made of

stone, looks enormous next to the squat flat-roofed huts
that line the narrow streets. The green pasture dotted with
palms is thriving thanks to the trickle of water that only
sometimes swells into a river. The sun never tires of falling
every day behind a steep and solitary mountain that
stretches from north to south between the two ranges that
define the valley. That one mountain, however, doesn't quite
span the width of the valley; through the remaining space
flows a trickle of water and every afternoon the twilight rays
of the sun king are projected through that opening onto the
facing moutains. And since these slopes are barren, without cacti or shrubs or *yaretas* or even a miserable mesquite
grove, they turn into enormous screens on which the sun
mixes colors as did Mondrian on his canvases. The world's
largest screen looks as if it were on fire, and at that moment
of the day nobody doubts that the desert has a few cards of
beauty hidden in its hand.

The night of San Lorenzo hosts the same wild and exuberant party of stars as in the rest of the desert pampa. It
begins discreetly when the sun has just gone to bed behind
the lifeless horizon. The stars emerge one by one across the
pampa ceiling, and by the time each one has obediently
taken the place it has held for millions of years, the dead
begin to emerge from their tombs.

III

When all was said and done, Justino Mamani was the
only local who took pity on the wandering souls of the
dead. He was eighty-eight years old, a tiny, shriveled man
with sunken cheeks and clouded vision. With little for
them to hang on, his pants were bound tightly around his

waist with an old belt. Rather than the flesh around bones that constitutes the body of a normal man, his pitiful anatomy was little more than bags of air. Don Justino's life, however, was powerfully supported by the ramparts of his spirit. Not one of life's blows had managed to destroy his desire to live, and he had the fathomless grace to exude joy wherever he went on his wrinkled, childlike feet. He had discovered the wondrous fact that all he had to do was light a candle in the village church on the day of the festivities of San Lorenzo in memory of a restless soul, and that soul would cease to roam aimlessly around the world of the living. In addition, and in order to convince the saint to forgive the sinner, he had to write the name of the deceased on the candle and recite repeatedly the sin or sins committed by the person in question. As a result of his diligence, for months now there had been only one ghost still roaming about under the obedient stars of San Lorenzo, and this is the one that gave don Justino the few gray hairs he had. There seemed to be simply no way to welcome into the realm of silence the ghost of someone who, in life, had been a German nomad.

Don Justino didn't know what sins that obstinate and irreverent man had committed, and no matter how many he invented, guessed at, contrived, and recited as he lay at the feet of the always obliging but forever demanding Saint Lorenzo, the dead man kept wandering around. All the locals got to know him, and if it weren't for the bad habit the dead have of stealing little bits of souls, they would have invited him for a game of dice or to share with them a glass of wine. Finally, purely by coincidence, and on the day he least expected it, don Justino learned the nature of the German's sins. As it turns out, the world is small, no matter how much it puffs itself up with its enormous mountain ranges or struts about vainly with its infinite deserts, huge jungles, or boundless oceans.

The well-known ghost had been a German world traveler named Fedor van der Kontje, who, while trying to take pictures of the religious celebration one day in San Lorenzo, stepped on a loose rock on the edge of the church tower and plunged into the void shouting a word that nobody understood: *Scheisseeeeeeeeeeee!* His death, however, was not in vain. His bulky gringo body fell squarely onto a sadistic pig who, during this country's recent past, had devoted himself to the despicable work of torturing political prisoners in order to obtain information.

"And don't think it was easy to help that miserable scoundrel find rest," don Justino explained. "It was as if all the dead had formed a union to prevent that sadist from joining them in the sacred fields of eternal rest. I finally had to bring a huge candle, one of those you have to carry on your shoulder, and read over and over again the names of everybody who had been arrested, disappeared, and executed here in the north, and pray for all of them, repeating that Arcadio Adolfo Schweitzer Malverde—because, to make matters worse, that was the bastard's name—deeply regretted the physical and psychic suffering he had caused. This was the only way to prevent Schweitzer Malverde from wandering around the town every night."

IV

Fedor was from Hamburg and had a certain slovenliness typical of those from the north; he was awkward on the dance floor, tight-fisted with money, passionless in love, and methodical in everything he did. He was tall and curved like a streetlight, had milky white skin that turned red in the desert sun, hair the color of corn silk, a forehead that grew broader as his hair retreated, a thin, drawn face, and a prominent jaw. Oddly enough, his eyes were as jet black as the darkest billiard ball, something as unusual in a true German as are blue eyes in a black African.

His passion was photography, and his serious vice took possession of him after he bought his first camera. If there ever was someone who went crazy in the sun, it was he. From a young age he perched on the roof of his building and strategically set up the tripod of his camera with a tele-photo lens—the eye of his soul—to face the neighborhood park, his eyes feasting joyously upon the naked pink breasts of young German women. He sighed deeply and lascivi-ously as his heart embarked on its crooked path. When he observed couples locked in wanton embraces, his feverish desire was to watch as they consumed their passion.

During those short summers of his youth he discovered the true nature of his desire: his greatest, his only pleasure was to be a hidden spectator to the act of love. He thus ded-icated himself to finding women who would have sex with others while he watched from the shadows. Things didn't go so badly for him until he met Marta, who refused to play the part of exhibitionist.

Marta's father was Chilean and her mother was German. She was small and her round face was sheathed, like a ball, in white skin. She had very black, stiff hair and brown puppy-dog eyes that made her look helpless, and she was dearly beloved in the Chilean community for her sweet good nature. Fedor mistakenly assumed she was all alone in the world and that it would be easy to make her fall in love with him so he could carry her off to his land of sexual fantasies. The opposite occurred, for Marta quickly carried Fedor into her world and got him interested in Latin American culture. He learned how to cook Chilean dishes, and the walls of his house were soon covered with pictures of Pablo Neruda, Che Guevara, and Salvador Allende. He listened to the music of Silvio Rodríguez, Atahualpa Yupanqui, Violeta Parra, and Amparo Ochoa, and he attended events held by the Latin American exile community. Just when he was about to tell her that he was going to study Spanish, the sun shone on Hamburg as it never had before, and the only thing he wanted was for Marta to lie out in the park with her breasts in the sun while he devoured her through his lens.

Frustrated in his efforts to get her to accept and understand his voyeurism, Fedor struck her. The Chileans who loved Marta repaid him with the worst beating of his life. Aching and with his heart torn to shreds by the definitive loss of Marta, he went to a psychologist to get help for his obsession. After many sessions, the psychologist confidently assured Fedor that while it was impossible to cure him of his inappropriate urge to spy on others, he could channel this need into other activities such as, for example, the observation of the exuberance of nature. Fedor listened, sold his entire arsenal of pornography, and took off on a long voyage through Latin America.

When he arrived at the festival of San Lorenzo, he had already spent four years wandering like a pilgrim around the American continent, and when he climbed the stone tower of his death to take photographs of the religious celebration, memories of Marta came strongly to his mind as he stepped carefully on each stair. Yes, suddenly he was remembering her vividly. "Why in hell did I want to force her to be with someone else while I watched?" he asked himself without, for the first time in his life, even one voyeuristic impulse in his body.

When he reached the top of the tower he placed his hand on the bell. Never had he felt such a strong desire to make love to a woman, to Marta. He felt truly in love with her. Having not seen her for four years, he loved her as never before. He felt himself full of a love so pure that he wanted to leave his body in the river's diaphanous waters, and arrive, like perfectly aged firewood, into her arms. Just moments before his death, he experienced a sudden love purer and more transparent than anything he had ever known. Already on the edge of the stone tower, he needed Marta as he had never needed any woman in his life. He wanted to close his eyes and open them in Hamburg. With shaking hands and choked by sobs, he took one step toward the edge, focused his lens on a cluster of believers, and snapped a picture, the last of his life. Then, adjusting his zoom, he focused in on a dance of the devil, and saw through his lens, almost flush up against his nose, Marta's round, white face. He saw her smiling, smiling at him as she often had before he struck her, and his first reaction was to take a step toward her. His heart bursting with desire, he stepped on a loose stone at the edge of the tower and clawed the air with his *scheisseeeeeeeee,* a shout of horror that was extinguished when he landed on the body of that despotic torturer.

V

For five years, the Teutonic ghost roamed around under the stars of San Lorenzo until the small world sent Marta's husband—a Chilean who married her after he participated in the beating that had changed Fedor's life—to San Lorenzo as part of a German television crew. He recognized Fedor's name on a wooden cross and wanted to get some flowers for the grave, having had, perhaps, some misgivings, along with the rest of the Chilean posse, that their response to the perverted German may have been a bit too severe.

"There aren't any real flowers in this town," an old woman told Marta's husband. "The only flowers in San Lorenzo are made of paper and don Justino makes them." And so it was that the cameraman came to tell don Justino everything he knew about Fedor. After that, the old man had only to buy a single candle to put an end to the tedious nightly wanderings of the ghost of the German voyeur.

Translated by Katherine Silver

The Señora of the Nightgowns
Hernán Rivera Letelier

STILL THINKING about his dead mother, Hidelbrando del Carmen got off the bus in front of the newspaper building. As occurred almost every Saturday morning, the newspaper was late, and the newsboys pitched pennies in the small courtyard while waiting for it to arrive.

In order to make sure no one got an unfair advantage, the large galvanized doors to the street were closed as soon as the newspapers arrived. Once the dispatcher had passed the bundles out, the assorted men, women, and children

---

HERNÁN RIVERA LETELIER *(1950–) was born in Talca and raised in a mining town in the Atacama desert. He achieved sudden critical and commercial success with the publication in 1994 of his first novel. He is one of Chile's most widely read and critically acclaimed writers, and his name is currently under consideration for the prestigious National Award for Literature. He lives with his wife and children in Antofagasta. This text is taken from his second novel,* Himno del ángel parado en una pata. *It is a day in the life of Hidelbrando del Carmen, a teenage boy raised by evangelical parents in a small mining town in the Atacama desert, who moved to Antofagasta with his father after his mother's death a few years before.*

---

who sold papers on the street crowded in front of the doors
so they could scatter into the street at the same time.

Under a sky dawning pastel blue (just like the room of the
Señora of the Nightgowns), with thirty-three newspapers
tucked under his arm and poised like a racehorse ready to gallop off the moment the bar was lowered, Hidelbrando del
Carmen waited impatiently among this odd assortment of
outlandish characters: greasy blind men with transparent skin
and dirty white hair; taciturn men with shifty eyes who were
missing a hand or a whole arm and attempted to hide their
stumps under their shabby rags; wheelchair-bound para-
plegics who sold women's magazines and lottery tickets as
well as newspapers; women, down on their luck, wearing blue
canvas shoes, soccer socks, and three or more torn sweaters
one on top of the other; and a whole bunch of bedraggled
children whose language was fouler than a drunken sailor's.

Of all these bizarre fauna, Hidelbrando del Carmen
always focused his attention on one man in particular. His
name was Andrés Onésimo Pitágoras Flores Moroso, and
every morning the dispatcher, in a loud voice and jesting
tone, called out his full name, and by way of a final and festive flourish, added, "alias, El Pita." El Pita was a small,
squat man who cackled horribly through a toothless grin,
and whom the others, especially the children, teased and
harassed mercilessly. The grimacing old man, with bow legs
and a nose as red as a berry, was little taller than a dwarf.
"Maybe you could call him a tall dwarf," Hidelbrando del
Carmen always mused to himself, remembering that this is
how he pictured Zachaeus, the tiny biblical character who,
in order to see Jesus in a crowd, climbed a sycamore tree
(how he liked the word *sycamore;* how pleasantly it echoed

in his ear every time he heard it read at church meetings). But it wasn't so much the cartoonlike appearance of this eccentric newsboy that caught his attention, but rather his certainty that he had seen him once in Algorta.

Ninety percent of the inhabitants of this mining town had come to live in Antofagasta when the mine shut down. The priest, a corpulent and vigorous man with black wiry hair and energetic gestures who punished the children in his religion classes—terrifying classes that he was allowed not to attend because his parents were evangelicals—by hitting them on the palms of their hands with wooden crucifixes, had managed to acquire some land at the foot of Cerro de la Cruz for all the homeless Algortinos. Obviously his parents had refused to register with the priest, and as a result, when they arrived in the city and while they were looking for a place to live, the pastor allowed them to build a lean-to on land belonging to the Evangelical church. Hidel-brando del Carmen was sure that El Pita was one of the many Algortinos who had emigrated to Antofagasta. He thought he remembered seeing him once dancing drunk-enly—it simply couldn't have been anyone else—at a party organized on the spur of the moment in the town's basketball stadium, which he had snuck into without his mother's permission. The little man, his red nose shining from alcohol, was making everybody laugh by dancing a *merengue apambichao*—the popular dance at the time—alone in the middle of the court accompanied by a haphazard orchestra comprised of people banging empty oil tins, blowing on combs wrapped in paper, and hitting empty beer bottles rhythmically with the skeleton keys that opened the doors to the single men's rooms.

The one thing Hidlebrando del Carmen didn't quite remember was if this had been at the bash the old folks had put together after a soccer match between the local team and the one from the port of Mejillones or the party held a few days before, following the big rally for the presidential candidate Salvador Allende Goosens during his second electoral campaign. At this sensational event, held in the same stadium, he had, for the first time in his life, seen a woman wearing slacks. Red, he remembered, without pockets, with a clasp on the side and flared at the ankles. And they were worn by none other than the young and beautiful wife of the candidate. He remembered her as clear as day because she was happy and enthusiastic that afternoon and had lead the crowd in the popular chant: "¡*Pica al ajo, pica al ají, sale Allende, claro que sí*"—"Chop the garlic, chop the chili, have no fear, Allende will win!"

A sharp elbow in his ribs brusquely awoke him from his reverie. It was none other than Pellizca la Luna. The giant forcefully pushed him out of the way and planted himself in front of him in a rude and openly provocative manner. As always when they rushed out of the building in a stampede, today he would again have to challenge this bully for the same route. During previous races they had run against each other, Pellizca la Luna had twice been on the verge of tripping him and sending him head over heels. "If that brainless bag of bones weren't quite so big . . . ," Hidelbrando del Carmen mused as he looked at him angrily from below, poised to attack.

When the doors were thrown open, Hidelbrando del Carmen took off running down Matta Street to the north. Despite Pellizca la Luna's threatening posture, he was going to take the same route he always did: he would go down Matta until he reached Prat Street; from there he would turn down Condell—always going north—until he reached Bolívar Street, which he would follow until he got to the fisherman's cove, where his route ended. Then, if he hadn't sold all his papers, he would go back downtown and stand at a bus stop to hawk whatever was left.

At first, the skinny bully with his daddy longlegs passed him and started hawking his papers aggressively. Hidelbrando del Carmen, following quickly upon his heels, crossed to the other side of the street. His tactic was to let the emaciated giant shout alone, let him rant and rave. Shouting was tiring, and he knew that they both didn't need to do it at the same time. Once in a while, and so as not to let the giant get too far ahead with his kangaroo hops, he would pass up a customer who was too slow or who didn't have the exact change ready.

As always, he let Pellizca la Luna keep his lead for the five blocks down Matta until they reached the Lucerna Bar, then down Prat for one block to the corner of Condell. Then, just as Hidelbrando del Carmen turned north, he began to sprint. He had to get ahead of his rival and stay ahead of him for two blocks before he reached Bolívar. Two blocks, by whatever means necessary. Reaching the fisherman's cove wasn't his goal, as his contender wrongly supposed, but rather reaching Bolívar first. To be more precise, to be the first to get to the block between Latorre and San Martín.

On Condell, almost at the corner of Sucre, the giant, who was approximately twenty yards ahead, was called over by a taxi driver. Hidelbrando del Carmen, paying no attention to a hoarse-voiced drunk who called to him from the doors of the beer hall, Cervecería La Gloria, ran with all his might and passed Pellizca la Luna. At last he reached Bolívar; without looking back, he turned down the street toward the sea and at the same moment began hawking his papers at the top of his lungs.

In the middle of the block, just past the old Hotel Chile-Grecia, someone called to him from the balcony of an old, tumbledown mansion, and Hidelbrando del Carmen, thrilled as could be, stopped in front of the building's large wooden double doors. Pretending to have a pebble or a nail in one of his shoes, he bent down and leaned against the doors. He heard the sound of the bolt being released by a cord from above and, a moment later, saw one of the heavy doors open a crack. He didn't go in. He kept pretending he had something in his shoe as he watched behind him out of the corner of his eye. Still holding his shoe in his hand, he watched the giant run past and barely managed to duck the large wad of spit aimed straight at his forehead that hit one of the doors. He put on his shoe, waited another moment, made sure nobody saw him, then quickly slipped into the house.

The old two-story mansion—much the worse for age—was one of the first to be built as a hotel in this steamy historic neighborhood, full of bars, small restaurants, and cafes for sailors around the customhouse. All of these luxurious mansions with elegant rooms and expansive lobbies, whose last vestiges of splendor were being devoured mercilessly by moths and termites, had become, with the passage of time and the painful demise of the nitrate, or white gold, mines, run-down rooming houses whose residents were less than reassuring.

As he climbed the wide staircase, whose rotten wood creaked and groaned noisily under each of his steps, Hidelbrando del Carmen, his heart beating furiously, had but one thought. What color nightgown—or negligé as his mother would say—would she be wearing: the black one, the red one, or the pink one? Personally he preferred the pink one. When he reached the wide landing on the second floor, he walked without hesitation toward the only open door, the one with the shiny, hand-polished brass doorknob. He pushed on it gently, using the hand in which he carried, as usual and already folded, three newspapers and, with bated breath, stuck in his black oil-slicked head. Bingo! It was the pink one.

The woman, standing next to a delicate round table in the middle of the room, outlined by the light that poured in through the windows behind her, was counting out a handful of coins she had emptied from a shiny black patent-leather purse and was carefully organizing them into neat piles of ten. A mirror, hanging on the door of the heavily varnished dark wardrobe, reflected a corner of her unmade bed, its red satin bedspread thrown shamelessly on the floor (just the sight of this bed produced in him a disturbing dizziness of fascination and fear) and reflected the full length of her nakedness shining through the transparent pink lace nightgown. She was a tall woman of indefinite age, her hair exquisitely disheveled à la Bardot and her angular, birdlike face wearing an enigmatic expression. She had tiny breasts, but it was her long legs shining golden through the generous opening in her gown that sent Hidelbrando del Carmen into a delirium of delight. Those gorgeous bronze legs, with the same hypnotizing brilliance as the doorknob, were comparable only to those of the heavenly Mexican movie star, Rosita Quintana.

The first time the woman's vague silhouette called to him from one of the upstairs windows of that old mansion, Hidelbrando del Carmen had climbed the stairs grumpily and reluctantly, regretting the precious time he was losing. But when, reticently, he entered the room painted in a crepuscular blue, he stood there dumbfounded. It had seemed to him that suddenly, as if by magic, after sneaking past the doorman and the usher of a mysterious private movie house, he had not only made his way right up to the rectangular screen, but had actually entered into an erotic scene of a French X-rated color film.

Since that first day, he had never failed to pass by this house. Sometimes, in the mornings, when he woke up and could barely drag himself out of bed, all he had to do was think about the possibility of the Señora of the Nightgowns beckoning to him to suddenly throw off the blankets and jump out of bed. Nonetheless, ever since he had been climbing up to the fragrant room of this solitary woman (if sin had a scent, Hidelbrando del Carmen was sure it was the perfume in that room), the only thing he had ever asked in a stammering voice was her name.

"Nymph Maria," she answered laconically.

Her voice, a hoarse whisper, sounded to him as if it rose from a seashell, one of those covered with mother of pearl he had seen natives blowing through in movies filmed on some Polynesian island. He wanted to ask her why she always bought three newspapers, but he couldn't find his voice.

There were times, however, when the curtains over the upper-story window of the mansion were not drawn back

and nobody called to him. On those occasions, Hidelbrando del Carmen would slow down, cup his hands over
his mouth, and hawk his newspapers with ever more vehemence. Anxiously glancing up at the windows, he would
shout over and over, each time more desperately. Imagining that the woman, after a long and wild night of partying, had simply overslept, he walked around the block and
passed by again, slowly, in vain, shouting at the top of his
lungs in front of the closed balcony. On those particular
days, his job seemed tedious, boring, and dreary, like a
movie that is pure dialogue.

When the woman finished counting out the coins, she
gestured, as always and with a slight toss of her head, for
him to enter the room. Hidelbrando del Carmen, also as
always, entered as if walking on air, with the same humility and devotion one assumes when entering a place of wor-
ship during a liturgy. Almost holding his breath, he placed
the folded newspapers on the small table with carved legs,
and in the sweaty palm of his open hand he received the
small piles of coins that she parsimoniously, almost sensu-
ously, placed there one at a time. Then, again as usual, without looking away from the woman who stared straight into
his eyes, Hidelbrando del Carmen began walking backward
toward the door. Sometimes, the woman's stare was mysterious and disturbing; at other times, it seemed hard and
mocking, like that of an evil blond bombshell in a movie;
and there were other days when her eyes distilled a delirious tenderness that made his body shake from head to toe
(and made him wonder if the Señora of the Nightgowns
was half-crazy). When he reached the threshold, Hidelbrando del Carmen avoided her eyes (today's look was that

of the evil blond), said thank you in an almost inaudible whisper, and left. As he ran down the stairs to the street, he realized that his whole body was in a sweat.

Old Bolívar Street, now full of hotels and rooming houses, was one of the few streets in the city with some history and was also known as the official street of the prostitutes. "The street of Sodom and Gomorrah," his mother would say when she mentioned the sinful Corrida del Medio in their hometown of Algorta.

Completely absorbed in his thoughts, Hidelbrando del Carmen made his way toward the fisherman's cove, crossing streets, avoiding cars, and hawking his newspapers almost in a daze. Come to think of it, he didn't think the señora looked at all like a prostitute. La Azuquita con Leche, the first whore he had ever met, with her squinty eyes and the scar from a knife wound across her cheek, definitely looked like one. At the intersection of Balmaceda Street, the screeching sound of a train coming from Bolivia cut his thoughts right down the middle.

As he watched the long train pass by on its way to the port, the engineer ringing the bronze bell as a warning, he suddenly saw, on the other side of the tracks, like a shimmering vision—and he kept seeing her intermittently between the cars as they passed—a beautiful albino girl distractedly contemplating the train's slow advance. The anemic seven o'clock sun shone resplendent off her white hair with a part of snow down the middle and made her pale skin look even more transparent. The little girl was wearing a white lacy dress, like one worn for the first holy communion, and in her hand she held a fragile package wrapped in paper (with two small horns) that he, instantaneously and unconsciously, assumed to be a kilo of white sugar.

When the endless cargo train finally passed, Hidelbrando del Carmen continued on his way toward the cove, again lost in his thoughts. Of course, Azuquita con Leche looked like a prostitute. On Sundays in the mining town, when his mother sent him to sell *empanadas* and bread in a straw basket covered with a piece of white cloth cut out of a flour bag, the first place he went was the Corrida del Medio, and the first room he visited was, of course, Azuquita con Leche's. Just the sight of the prostitute fascinated him. Contemplating the livid stitches of the scar on her cheek seemed as immodest as looking at her sex.

One cloudy Sunday (he never understood why memorable things always happened to him on cloudy days) he had seen another woman in Azuquita con Leche's room singing a Mexican *corrida*. That was the only time he saw her, but her voice (not her face) had been etched forever into his memory. Sitting on the edge of her unmade bed, accompanied on the guitar by one of the drunken late-night revelers, she sang a *ranchera* in the same languid tone the evangelical sisters sang the church hymns. The song, he found out later, was called "La Calandria," and every time he heard it he remembered that small woman with hazy features whom one of the drunken men, as he offered her an *empanada*, called by the strange nickname, La Reina Isabela.

Translated by Katherine Silver

The Train

Roberto Ampuero

THE WOOD HOUSE was small and the dining room window faced the open pampa. The train passed right in front, once in the morning and once in the afternoon. After the train had gone, the place again grew calm and the nervous leaves settled down as the noise faded into joyful clattering. Then peace and silence returned.

Pedro often walked out to the tracks with a bucketful of dirt.

"Shitheads!" he exclaimed to himself as he poured the contents over the excrement deposited on the ties.

He returned to his house mumbling unintelligibly, crossed his patio where a grapevine grew, hung the bucket next to the flowerpots, and entered the kitchen.

He lived alone and far from the village. He had no com-

ROBERTO AMPUERO *(1953–) was born in Valparaíso and began his literary career in Chile in 1993 with the publication of a novel that won* El Mercurio *newspaper's prestigious Best Novel Prize. Ampuero has since published several more books, including a series of detective novels, and is one of Chile's best-selling contemporary writers. He currently lives and teaches in Iowa.*

pany other than an old, half-blind dog and a goldfinch
that had begun to lose its feathers. He asked for nothing
more than what he already had and that the inspectors
close the bathrooms on the train before they got to his
place.

"I must go talk to the switchman in the village," he said
to himself as he soaked the onions. "Maybe he'll understand."

One spring morning, he decided to go see the switchman.

"What do you want, Pedro?" asked the railroad man
without raising his eyes from the shoe he was mending.

"I want you to listen to me, Anselmo."

The old man continued to inspect the sole of his shoe.
The sun entered obliquely through the window and bathed
the room in light. There were several large stopped clocks
in the room, which was filled with the smell of paraffin.

"I listen with my ears, Pedro," the switchman reminded
him and turned the shoe on his knee.

Pedro looked out the window. The dew was already
shimmering between the rocks. He cleared his throat and
again turned his small eyes toward the old man. For an
instant he despised his dark cap and his hands with their
fat fingers.

"I like people to look me in the eyes when I talk."

"And people talk into my ears when I am fixing my shoes
and lowering the crossing gate," said the old man as he lowered his face even more.

"I came about the train."

"The morning train or the afternoon train?"

"Both."

"What do you want? For it not to pass in front of your house?"

"No."

"For it to stop making noise?"

Pedro didn't answer. He waited for the old man to look at him, but it was in vain. The railroad man continued, immersed in his work.

"What's the problem, then? Are they burning your carnations?"

"They fill my patio with shit," Pedro answered as he blushed and turned to look out at the open pampa.

"You aren't the only one."

"What?"

"Some more, some less, everybody gets some from somebody. Everyone shits on someone some time. There's no shit that doesn't have a target, Pedro."

The old man delicately placed his shoe on a chair and picked the other one up from the floor.

"The important thing is not to drown in it, Pedro. In this country, it's up to our ears."

Pedro cleared his throat again.

"But I can't spend my life burying other people's shit, Anselmo."

"You're wrong, Pedro, you can, until the day you die."

"There's no way, then? How about closing the bathrooms before they get to town?"

"No, Pedro, people are free to shit whenever they want."

Pedro looked out into the distance as if searching for a solution. The entire pampa was shimmering.

"So, there is no possible solution?" he asked after a long silence.

"No, Pedro, there isn't."

"I'll go then, Anselmo."

"Nope, there's no solution," the old man repeated and he raised his green eyes to watch Pedro walking away along the dirt road. Then he slowly got up; it was time for the train.

Translated by Katherine Silver

Afternoon in the Pampa

Roberto Ampuero

THEY STOOD VERY QUIETLY next to the contraption, listening to the hurricane-like screech of the wind. They were on their knees among the thorny thistles hanging on to their straw hats as the sun began to descend, setting the cracked earth on fire.

"It's not going to work," the boy said.

"It has to rise: it's shaped like the wings of a bird," the old man answered.

"Yeah, but the one we made in September was too."

The old man appeared not to have heard what he said and began to examine every knot and nail that held the wood and cardboard together. The contraption was twice as tall as he was, and each wing was at least a yard wide. He had painted the whole thing green, like the forests of the south.

"Come on," the boy ordered, "we've got to take out the rocks."

After removing the ballast, they grabbed their contraption by the wings and lifted it into the air; it wanted to take off, but they held on to it tightly and began walking. Their rubber sandals sank into the dirt, and the wind inflated their clothes like balloons and threatened to blow off their hats.

At the foot of the hill they paused but did not speak to each other. The old man inspected the contraption with excited eyes while the boy observed the sky as it began to grow dark. Then they started climbing, their sandals slipping on sharp rocks, their torsos sweating, their tired legs shaking. Out of breath, they reached the top and looked down on the village with its little adobe houses and empty streets.

"Get in," the old man said as he spit out grains of sand.

The boy got into the contraption and helped carry it into position. He closed his eyes.

"One, two, three . . ." the old man counted, and his jugular vein seemed about to pop out of his turkeylike neck.

They took off running down the hill, huffing and puffing, their lungs about to burst, until the old man shouted, "Now!" and let go. The boy ran on his tiptoes a few more yards, the green body rose lightly and gently for a few seconds, as if ready to take off flying over the entire desert pampa, then fell on its side with its passenger and rolled slowly down the hill before coming to a complete stop.

"Shit," said the old man.

The boy emerged from between the broken boards and torn cardboard; a trickle of blood ran down the back of his hand; he had lost his hat.

"It fell apart," he said, sucking his blood.

The old man looked disconsolately at the remains.

"What now?" the boy asked, his lips tinted red.

"Back to town, start all over again," the old man answered as the boy put on his hat.

Again they carried the contraption, though it seemed lighter now that it was in pieces and offered less wind resistance. They walked with their heads down, in silence, each one lost in his own thoughts, as if they were indifferent to the weight they carried.

"Look at that!" the boy shouted, his eyes glued on the sky.

The old man slowly lifted his head and observed the blue dome for interminable seconds, then his eyes came to rest on the path. His only answer was the crunching of the gravel under his sandals.

"But the night will catch him up there," the boy said a moment later looking over at the old man through the slats. He heard him clear his throat and spit against the warm rocks.

Above, the silver lamina reflecting the last light of the afternoon had already disappeared.

Translated by Katherine Silver

Walking the Atacama

Luis Alberto Acuña

WHEN THE INFERNAL SUN pounds down on your head, hangs from your shoulders, and tackles you around the knees, you can feel how it's trying to smash you to the earth face first, bloody your forehead, and make you swallow the dry, acid soil through your busted teeth.

You walk and walk along the track with your eyes glued to the ground because there's nothing to see. It's all the same ahead, behind, and to the sides except for the narrow track like a long scar across the desert, broken sometimes or covered by stretches of sand.

You walk and walk with worn-out steps like you're going nowhere . . . or will never get there, because it's hours and hours and days and days. Sometimes you look back for no reason, like you might be hearing the sound of a motor and you're looking for the dust cloud that

LUIS ALBERTO ACUÑA *was born in Iquique and has published five volumes of stories and novels. He has received numerous literary prizes including the Santiago Municipal Prize. One of his stories was recently made into a short film for the Chilean National Television Network, and many of his works have been anthologized in Chile and in other countries.*

would give it away. Maybe that truck won't stop, but maybe the next one will, and there you'll be with your bones rattling and your elbow leaning against the rail of the truck, or your legs dangling off the back and your ass getting kicked by every pothole in the road. If it's not a big truck, just a pickup, then you'll amuse yourself dragging your old boots in the sandy soil. Maybe the ride lasts a couple of hours, then you hop off, wave your thanks and good-bye, and go back to slogging along the track again. Maybe this time you won't have to walk far, you'll get picked up right away. Maybe you'll even be lucky enough to get invited to ride in the cab. They'll want you to talk, but after the cigarette, if you've been walking a long time, you'll nod off right in the seat.

So it goes, little by little, until you finally arrive. And then, almost always, the tip turns out to be false. The mine is already shut down or else they're planning to close it and there isn't even a hope of a job. On the road again, following another tip, passing through ghost towns where with luck there are a few old folks, a few kids and dogs still around. Or you're out of luck, because all the tin shacks are gone and there's not even a watchman left to guard the place, because the plant has moved away, skin and bones and all, and thieves have taken even the rusty nails so all that's left are graves. There's just a cemetery like an island in the middle of the desert. A cemetery with dry, cracked crosses, no hint of color. A dead cemetery, slapped down there by some mysterious hand, offering you no protection from the noonday sun or sharp nighttime cold. A cemetery where, if you took it into your head to dig, you'd find a corpse intact as if they'd buried it last week, even though the funeral was twenty years ago. Dry, for sure, and turned yellow, or maybe brown.

Suppose you took a notion to water it, so it could soak up some moisture, and swell, and grow soft, so it wouldn't have to be as dry as the earth all around it, so it could rot away like any other corpse. Suppose you took such a notion, how could you manage that? Pissing on it would be ugly, and you're not going to waste the water in your canteen, because tomorrow you might be as stiff as your friend there, stretched out in the middle of the pampa, if you took a notion to leave the track and strike out cross-country to save time. Nobody could water you even if they found you, because lying on top of the ground you wouldn't be shrunken up like a mummy, you'd just be a pile of yellowed bones. Anyway, even if you watered the stiff every day, where are the organisms that are going to make him rot? The noonday sun would kill them, and so would the midnight cold. The corrosive nitrate would burn them up.

Hit the road again, my friend, walk the track once more. If there's not going to be a truck, then it's better to start in the evening, walk through the night 'til dawn. Protect your body from the hammering sun, and let walking keep out the cold. Walking, your teeth don't chatter or your muscles seize up like they do when you're curled under your blanket, trying to sleep.

You walk and walk. Sometimes for hours, 'til a truck comes by . . . and stops for you. Well, that's how it used to be. Now, with the Panamerican Highway, the desert is overrun with vehicles—even minibuses, if you've got the money to pay the fare. But you haven't got any money, because the work ran out. For you, and for everybody else. There aren't any buses that run north-south, there isn't any Panamerican Highway, just the long insufferable track, covered in stretches by sand, that connects one nitrate mining town with the next.

Sometimes, pal, you'll come upon a village when your canteen has been dry for hours, the sun has baked your brains, your eyes are bloodshot, and your swollen tongue is like a dirty rag in your mouth. There's always one lone little house at the edge of the village, where they'll give you water and you can recover your strength.

You smell the water from far off, you guess that it's evaporating from a sink where an old woman is doing her washing, and the tiny droplets are floating to your nose.

You have to get closer and lean your arms on the little fence of old boards that holds back the desert just enough to make a yard for the house. You have to smile at the old lady and greet her politely. "Good afternoon, señora, could you spare me a little water . . . you old bitch? May I wash off in that bucket, if you could be so kind, because I'm so hot and dusty . . . and I smell as bad as you!"

While you wash you look at the clothes on the line, so white, because she's put a little bleach in her rinse. Just to think that you could possibly sleep in a bed with sheets that white!

Now that you've taken off your sweaty shirt and thrown water on your head and chest, now that you've cooled down and slaked your thirst, hunger hits you next. You've got to make more conversation to see if you can bring her round. If her husband was home, he'd invite you to sit down and eat something, unless maybe both of them are sick of all the men swarming through, like ants, looking for work in the mines.

But maybe the woman's alone, because the guy took off
or died or is working in another town. Maybe he had to go
down to Iquique to see the grandniece who was about to
have a baby there. Then she might not want to trust you,
she might look you in the eye and claim she hasn't got any
food while she dries her wrinkled hands on that apron she
wears. If she looks deeper in your eyes, she might see a solid
working man who's just out of a job, not because he's lazy
but because times are bad and every month another mine
shuts down. A tired man, but a good one, even if his growth
of whiskers gives him a shady look, especially if you've
washed up and that layer of dirt is gone from your face.
Then the old lady might take pity, because she's got a son
you remind her of or who knows why else. So you might
get a good meal after all. A thick stew with big chunks of
potatoes that'll burn your tongue because you can't wait for
them to cool down after you cut them in half. Even a glass
of wine from a bottle she's been saving in the cupboard,
which she serves you while she goes on and on about herself and the village and everything, because once they get
over their suspicions women turn into blabbermouths.

Then maybe the old woman will pour herself a glass of
wine, too, to keep you company, though she hardly ever
drinks because it raises her blood pressure and gives her a
headache she can only get rid of by lying down and going
to sleep with those cork-paper cigarette butts pasted to her
temples with spit. And you, after you've had a few more
glasses, realize she isn't looking at you like she'd look at a
son any more, but in a different way, like the young man you
are. Old bitch, dirty old lady, what are you thinking about?
Does she think just because she gave you something to eat

you have to repay her with some of that? Maybe you get
pissed, because the sun baked your brains so long and the
wine is making your insides buzz. Maybe you get an evil
flash that reminds you the next house is pretty far away and
nobody has seen you yet. Reminds you how you spotted a
roll of bills behind the wine bottle in the cupboard . . . and
you don't have a red cent to your name.

The old lady coming on to you like a nanny goat. The
devil wrapping somebody's hand around the bottle and lift-
ing it up to smash it down on somebody else's skull. You see
the woman stretched out on the floor with her eyes wide
open and a pool of blood under her head, and you're para-
lyzed with fear. Because it happened against your will,
because all of a sudden that damn pampa got to you,
devoured you body and soul, changed you from a solid
working man to a murderer. A murderer who stands still,
listening, terrified, in case somebody outside could have
heard the body thump when it fell. Who realizes that
nobody has seen him and he better hit the road, better go
back the way he came or keep on ahead, but out in the open
desert now, because he's got to stay off the beaten track
where the *carabineros* will come to look for him.

You know you have to wipe out any trace of your presence, and you know, although you've always been a bum,
that this death was pointless because there aren't even a
hundred pesos in that roll of bills.

Or, maybe that isn't what happens at all. Maybe your
anger washes right through you, gone as fast as it came, and
you figure the poor old thing has gone a long time without
it, and you haven't had much chance either lately, so you'll
do her that favor in return for the plate of stew. You close

your eyes as if you had a blindfold over your face, close your
ears to her grunts of pleasure, make believe you're going to
bed with Teruca, who you haven't seen in a long time. Maybe you wonder how she's doing in Antofagasta, or maybe
you pretend it's that stuck-up princess who wouldn't even
give you the time of day, even though your nostrils quivered
at her perfume when you went by, at her perfume and the
scent of her skin.

There's always the sun pounding down on your head as
you walk along the track, always that thirst when your canteen runs dry. There's always an old woman, *compadre*, on
the outskirts of a village, out in her yard doing the wash if
the village hasn't died yet. There are always evil notions cir-
cling through your head, and sometimes they get out of
control.

Anything can happen in the desert, my friend.

Translated by Dick Cluster

-{ Concepción }-

Deputies' Street
Tito Matamala

I COULD NEVER AVOID that damn street with its sand sidewalks, buses tearing up and down, and collective taxis weaving in and out like rats at an elephant fight, nor could I avoid reading the graffiti on the walls that still proclaim the coming of the revolution, comrade, and that the working class will take power, and that hydroelectricity is the opiate of the people, you can see I memorized it all by going time and again down that street of infamy that gives off an early warning stench of the port of Talcahuano—what an ugly town—and is decorated with black trash bags that Mister Mayor hopes will be nicely piled up before they're picked up, trash street, trash-can soul, I say every time necessity forces me to go down that street on which a thousand years ago walked a woman made of

TITO MATAMALA *(1963–) was born in Puerto Montt and has lived in Concepción since 1982. He has published six books, and his stories have appeared in many anthologies. His last book, a collection of humorous essays,* Nuevo manual del buen bebedor, *was published in 2002. In addition to writing fiction, he works as a journalist and teaches at the Universidad de Concepción.*

white wax with hooks for hands and melted-butter eyes, a
woman who melted me, intoxicated me, it was like wad-
ing through a deep, wide river of muscatel, a river almost
as wide as that nasty street that should be closed down,
Mister Mayor, I proclaim every so often, and the local
council pays me as much heed as that woman who devoured my books, drank from my overflowing cup of
wine, nibbled on my ears, and then as if nothing had ever
happened, took off in a taxi down that detested street on
which she lived in a government-issue, matchbox-sized
apartment, dazed by the burning smokestack of her own
being, her very foundation twisted by the sway of a black
heart sheathed in the white skin that she let me touch a
few times, and this was enough to cause the downfall of
my hands, they never rested easy again, not even now, as I
clutch the rail in the bus, looking at the opposite side of
the road, not her side, feeling bitterness in every rib at
having to float over that miserable, damned street ever
since she turned up with her suitcases, her all-black
outfits, and her army of ashtrays she had trained never to
complain, so then how could I complain, after falling into
the tomb of her castle one April afternoon, back when I
still believed you could sin without being seen, without
having to answer to your guts for all eternity on that street
that Mister Mayor never sees fit to sweep, only to dig up
every so often so we don't lose the fighting spirit of a people at war, on the verge of collapse and of permanent
progress, as the President says, but Mister Governor, he's
not worried, because the streets aren't his responsibility,
speak to my friend the Mayor, ask him to take a stroll
down Colón Street, and of course he never does, because

the only idiot condemned to navigate through it is me, which wouldn't really matter, except that I also used to walk down it with that woman whose wrought-iron heart I sensed the very first day she raised the bridge of her nose to me, but having a good eye for the devil does no good, because you might recognize him but you still fall, come on, admit it, and it does no good to know that you can't pay that check, that you mortgage your entire life away, just like me, here on this tin-can minibus where I feel my bones shake, my heart break, and a big stake was driven into the regulation corner of my soul on the unforgettable day I found myself driven from her matchbox castle overlooking the street of my eternal rage, the street I travel down today, my head condemned to look forever to the left so that my eyes don't happen accidentally upon the happy memories of the right side, where stands the little apartment like a smoking car on a train of that woman, that black-hearted woman who once opened the door to me and then closed it again, leaving me outside, you stay there, and I stayed there like the coward I am, cowardly but proud, drinking cheap moonshine, no lucky star for me, just contraband rum or sour-apple liquor, anything so as not to remember that I have to go down the street of destruction regardless, that street whose walls the deputies plaster over just before the elections with loads of truths and promises, loads of reconciliation, loads of regionalism—just after they get back from the capital—so that the street can then take on its pathetic gray air once again, similar to my own when I used to walk down its sand sidewalks to the sea-blue-eyed woman's cave and knock on her door knowing she wouldn't let me in, just like that, that's how it happened, I tell myself as I ride the Club Hípico-Hualpencillo minibus, plowing through the plains of her domains, spineless as the third-rate coward I've always been and trying to deny the wicked memory of that woman with Chinese silk scarves, carmine-colored nails, and polyurethane skin who almost took my life the first time I followed her down Pelantaro, Chacabuco, Prat, 21 de Mayo, and Colón, until I lost my soul in the whitewater of misfortune that this reputable street represents for me, this street that I am obliged to travel almost every day, craning my neck to the left and my soul to hell, but I swear that today is the last day, that today I will look to the right and see her bitter memory, venomous woman, I say, and all I manage to see in the oft-traveled distance, in her apartment window, is a sad little sign that says For Rent.

Translated by Lisa Dillman

The Chilean Forest

Pablo Neruda

UNDER THE VOLCANOES, beside the snow-capped mountains, among the huge lakes, the fragrant, the silent, the tangled Chilean forest . . . My feet sink down into the dead leaves, a fragile twig crackles, the giant rauli trees rise in all their bristling height, a bird from the cold jungle passes over, flaps its wings, and stops in the sunless branches. And then, from its hideaway, it sings like an oboe . . . The wild scent of the laurel, the dark scent of the boldo herb, enter my nostrils and flood my whole being . . . The cypress of the Guaitecas blocks my way . . . This is a vertical world: a nation of birds, a plenitude of leaves . . . I stumble over a rock, dig up the uncovered hollow, an enormous spider covered with red hair stares up at me, motionless, as huge as a crab . . . A golden carabus beetle blows its mephitic breath at me, as its brilliant rainbow disappears like lightning . . . Going on, I pass through a forest of ferns much taller than I am: from their cold green eyes sixty tears splash down on my face and, behind me, their fans go on quivering for a long time . . . A decaying tree trunk: what a treasure! . . . Black and blue mushrooms have given it ears, red parasite plants have

149

covered it with rubies, other lazy plants have let it borrow their beards, and a snake springs out of the rotted body like a sudden breath, as if the spirit of the dead trunk were slipping away from it . . . Farther along, each tree stands away from its fellows . . . They soar up over the carpet of the secretive forest, and the foliage of each has its own style, linear, bristling, ramulose, lanceolate, as if cut by shears moving in infinite ways . . . A gorge; below, the crystal water slides over granite and jasper . . . A butterfly goes past, bright as a lemon, dancing between the water and the sunlight . . . Close by, the innumerable calceolarias nod their little yellow heads in greeting . . . High up, red copihues (*Lapageria rosea*) dangle like drops from the magic forest's arteries . . . The red copihue is the blood flower, the white copihue is the snow flower . . . A fox cuts through the silence like a flash, sending a shiver through the leaves, but silence is the law of the plant kingdom . . . The barely audible cry of some bewildered animal far off . . . The piercing interruption of a hidden bird . . . The vegetable world keeps up its low rustle until a storm churns up all the music of the earth.

Anyone who hasn't been in the Chilean forest doesn't know this planet.

I have come out of that landscape, that mud, that silence, to roam, to go singing through the world.

Translated by Hardie St. Martin

Black Bird

Marta Brunet

WE HAD SPENT THE WHOLE morning and afternoon
on narrow mountain paths only wide enough for one
abreast, remaining always watchful of the horses' precarious footing.

We were following the riverbed from high above. The
sheer cliffs and jagged, rocky peaks rose above us, enormous
and gray, thick green patches clinging to the ledges, waterfalls fed by melting snows making their thunderous descent,
and steep cliffs covered with moss. The air was cold and
opaque. You could see the setting sun reverberating on the
peaks, and its warm rays, which one could only imagine,
made the freezing dampness of our path unbearable.

I began to feel overwhelmed with exhaustion. Every
once in a while I would ask the guide, "How much farther
have we to go?"

MARTA BRUNET *(1897–1967) was born in Chillán. She was
a diplomat, journalist, and a key figure in Chilean literary and intellectual circles. She is considered one of the founders of the* criollista
*school because of her portrayals of the landscape, rural life, and the psy-
chological subjectivity of her characters, especially women. She received
the prestigious National Literary Award in 1961.*

And the man would invariably respond, "Just around the corner, m'lady."

Knowing, as I do, what "just around the corner" means to a highlander, I didn't have much faith that the house where we were going to spend the night—the home of a rural postman who had some business dealings with my father—was close by. We were on our way to a lost lake nestled in among the volcanoes of the Malleco province; a painter friend of mine had described it to me, extolling its beauty.

At one spot, the path became so dangerous that we were forced to dismount and continue on foot. A flock of birds was perched on the cliffs, so high above us that they looked like dots, shadow stars in the iridescent sky. One of the peons said:

"Vultures just biding their time 'til somebody slips and they come an' eat 'im."

I could feel the hard curved beak digging into my flesh. I grew frightened and anxiously repeated my question.

"How much farther have we to go?"

With a reassuring smile, the guide answered, "Just around the corner, m'lady."

"But this corner never comes . . . and night is approaching. . . . Anything could happen."

"Aw, nothing'll happen, and if it does, well, it was meant to be—destiny wanted it to. But trust me, mistress, we'll see the house from right over there."

I shrugged my shoulders in doubt and mounted my horse.

Tattered veils of blue began to float over the river, moving slowly until they touched each other and fused, forming a single shadow that climbed the cliffs, penetrated the hollows, tangled in the brambles, and rose slowly but steadily until it covered the peaks. The summer night with its turquoise radiance had arrived, and the stars, like silver tacks, seemed to shiver in the sky.

"There's the house," the guide said, pointing to a light on the flank of the mountain.

We had just finished eating. Sitting by my side, the woman of the house was meticulously preparing *mate* tea. She was in her fifties and must have been beautiful when she was young. Only a few small wrinkles encircled her extraordinarily bright, expressive eyes, which seemed to emit some kind of green brilliance. She spoke with animation, and her movements betrayed a certain nervous vehemence. It was clear that she was the axis on which that house turned. Her husband hardly uttered a word. He looked like a typical small-town businessman with a rectangular frame, a pot belly, and a big head, hands, and feet. There were nine children, all girls, an array of innocuous faces, with no charm other than their apple-toned skin and frank eyes like their father's, gray and watery behind long lashes. All nine of them stood in a group behind their mother, their eyes turned down yet full of curiosity, wanting to look, stealing a peek out of the corners of their eyes, then quickly lowering them whenever they met mine. The youngest was about eight years old and sat on a hand-woven rug on the floor, staring at me with pupils like those of a small animal—dilated, fixed, soulless. She was the only one who looked directly at me without any shyness. When my eyes met hers, I smiled. She didn't seem to see my smile. The fixed expression on her face never changed.

I had had an hour of rest while they finished preparing the food, and I felt completely refreshed; my hunger made the food especially delicious. All my senses were fully alert, and feeling so alive, I was secretly happy.

We were outside in front of the kitchen of the little house, in the heart of the mountains, the immense night all around us as we huddled around a small bundle of flames.

The woman offered me some *mate*. I took slow sips between bites of bread and cheese.

A black bird flew slowly overhead, tracing large circles.

"A vulture," I said, and watched it until it disappeared in some trees.

When I turned to look at the family, I saw anxiety in every face. It was as if the bird had left behind a trail of dread.

"Was it a vulture?" I asked.

"Maybe, but I don't think so. Vultures are never alone. . . ."

The bird itself answered by raising its voice, which sounded like a dog's howl or the rattling laughter of a madman. Or the sound of a siren calling for help.

"Jesus!" the woman exclaimed. Suddenly and with surprising alacrity, she got up, went into the kitchen, returned with a fistful of salt, and threw it into the fire.

"Salt's tossed, evil's lost," they all said with the same anguish in their voices.

"Hail Mary, full of grace, the Lord is with you. Blessed are you among women, and blessed is the fruit of your womb, Jesus."

"Holy Mary, Mother of God, pray for us sinners, now and at the hour of our death. Amen."

"Salt's tossed, evil's lost."

"Salt's tossed, evil's lost."

After repeating these words three times, they explained to me what they were doing.

"It's the *chonchón*."

"It's a witch."

"*Chonchón* . . . , witch . . . ," I replied, stupefied, more by their explanation than by what had just occurred.

"Yes," the woman said, "they are witches who turn into birds on Saturday nights so they can perform evil deeds; they turn into *chonchones* and screech over the houses they will bring evil down upon. This one has already come several times, but it never finds us unprepared; immediately we chant the incantation, the counterspell, and it is forced to leave."

"But this is all foolishness."

"I also used to think as you do, ma'am. But we have had such a sad experience. . . ."

"What happened?"

"Look at this poor creature. She was cursed by a witch who lived in Montaña Negra, cursed before she was even born," and she pointed to the little one, still sitting on the ground with crossed legs, her little hands in her lap, and her eyes wide open and staring.

"Is she sick?"

"She is . . . innocent," and the mother's hand caressed the girl's head but got no reaction. "When I was first pregnant with her, Arturo, my husband, had a falling out with doña Bernarda, an old woman who had a reputation for being a bad person, some kind of half-healer/half-witch, who helped cattle rustlers and thieves, greedy, even capable of committing a crime if paid enough. The problem with Arturo began when a few of his calves disappeared, and he followed their footprints to Montaña Negra, right onto doña Bernarda's homestead. Arturo told her that if she didn't return the calves immediately he was going to go to the local sheriff. The old woman insisted that she knew nothing and had seen nothing. So Arturo went and got the sheriff and returned with him. The old woman continued to insist that she knew nothing about it. Nobody had ever been able to prove anything against her because she was so cunning, a real she-devil. But this time she didn't get away with it because Arturo didn't rest until finally he found the calves on her property, hidden away in the mountains. They arrested her, but not before she swore to take revenge against my husband, make him regret for the rest of his life that he had turned her in.

"As I said, I was already expecting. One night, a short time later, we heard the shout of the *chonchón* over our house. We thought nothing of it because we didn't believe in witches. The next morning I woke up sick—my whole body ached, and my head was bursting. I couldn't get out of bed. When I tried to stand up, everything spun around and I passed out. I continued like that for a week, then the *chonchón* flew over the house again. It was a Saturday night. I got frightened and I called to my husband.

"'What do you think,' I said, 'could it be doña Bernarda? They say she's a witch.'

"Arturo laughed. He called me silly. I was sick for another week and getting worse by the day. I couldn't keep any food down. And I trembled at the thought that Saturday would come again and the *chonchón* would return. Saturday came and the *chonchón* began to screech. Then I got a high fever and was so sick that Arturo got scared and called one of my sisters, a schoolteacher who knows a lot about remedies and witchcraft. He told her what had happened. I kept getting sicker. The following Saturday, they thought I was going to die. I was unconscious and gasping for breath. My sister showed my husband what to do. He prepared a dagger by holding it in the fire then sprinkling it with holy water. When night came, and the moon rose (it has to be a moonlit night), Arturo and my sister hid over there in those Maqui berry bushes and waited for the *chonchón*. The bird began to circle slowly overhead. All of a sudden the moon cast the shadow of the bird on the ground and my sister, as quick as lightning, thrust the dagger into the shadow and said, 'Salt's tossed, evil's lost,' and my husband repeated, 'Salt's tossed, evil's lost.'

"And they recited the Hail Mary three times, like we did just now. And the bird disappeared, just vanished into thin air.

"My sister ran into the house like a madwoman and hugged me and kissed me and reassured me that now I would get better, and she told me that the *chonchón* would not return, that the old woman was dead, that she would never again do evil to anybody. I listened to her and felt so refreshed by her words, so relieved.

"The next day I woke up without a fever. Two days later I was able to get out of bed. My sister came and danced with happiness, and we asked everybody who passed by for news of doña Bernarda, but nobody had heard any news of her. All we knew was that she had been back at home for a while because the sheriff had let her out on bail.

"A week passed. Saturday came and I found myself getting a little scared. Might the *chonchón* come again? I didn't sleep a wink, but all night I didn't hear a single screech. What a relief! The next day, I couldn't do anything but laugh and sing, and my sister the same, and even Arturo, who is usually so quiet, was like us, talkative and happy.

"The same day, some muleteers from the other side of Montaña Negra passed by.

"'What's new?' my sister asked them.

"'Doña Bernarda died suddenly. Exactly a week ago, she was found dead in her bed. When she didn't get up in the morning, her daughters went and found her stiff and cold. Her heart must've burst, 'cause she had a huge bruise on her chest.'

"We didn't say anything. Only afterward, and very quietly, we talked a bit among ourselves. We prayed and sprinkled holy water all around. We were very frightened that the old woman's soul would come after us. But such an evil soul must be in the deepest depths of hell and could never return. Finally we calmed down.

"But the girl was born and grew and grew, and you can see for yourself, ma'am. . . . That's how she is, like a baby, doesn't speak, barely even recognizes me . . . and she's already eight years old. She's the one who paid! The innocent one! And it's been about a month now that we've been feeling the *chonchón* again. We think it might be doña Bernarda's eldest daughter, who's getting a reputation for being as evil as her mother. But she can't do anything to us, because the minute we feel her coming, we say the prayer. You see, ma'am, how sad it is. Poor child!" and the mother's hand, more insistently, reached out to caress the unmoving head.

Then the little one turned slowly, and her unblinking eyes stared at her mother, down whose face ran a tear into the corner of her sad mouth.

We don't speak. I pass the *mate* back to the woman. Until the *mate* has made its way all around the circle, nobody speaks. The fire barely crackles. Above, the stars, like silver tacks, continue to shine tremulously.

Translated by Katherine Silver

—{ Aysén }—

Window on the South

Enrique Valdés

IT WAS THE FOURTH TIME my mother had sent me to Mrs. Leonta's house to ask for a bowl of flour, and she instructed me, "Tell her we will return it when winter is over."

"This has to be the last one," Mrs. Leonta answered, "because I'm also running low."

I was just beginning to understand what it meant to live here, in the middle of nowhere, where it seemed as if everything had recently been invented.

The house was only half-finished when we moved into it. My father built it little by little, and it grew as fast as he could bring from Coyhaique cross-grained boards and planks for the floor in those small airplanes that landed

ENRIQUE VALDÉS *(1943–) was born in Río Baker in the extreme south of Chile. He received his doctorate from the University of Illinois and taught at Purdue University. He had been awarded numerous prizes for his four novels, three volumes of poetry, and a volume of stories. He is currently professor of Latin American and children's literature at Universidad de Los Lagos in Osorno where he also directs a Chamber music ensemble.*

sporadically in Lago Verde. The first thing I missed was the stove my mother had used for cooking and baking bread. It was too big and heavy to carry on a horse's back all the way here. My father solved this problem his own way. He found an old oil drum discarded on the airfield and took it to the blacksmith to have some holes bored in it—one hole for the pipe and another for the door. A thick piece of sheet metal that divided the can in half was used as a base for the fire. This became the smoking stove my mother used daily for cooking. On it she made us deep-fried *sopaipillas* every day. And, just for a change, she would make *tortillas de rescoldo*.

Just as there are no roads between towns, there are also no streets in the town. Our house is built in the middle of a huge green field with wild plants and trees growing all around it. Farther away, scattered around the valley, are some twenty small houses that make up the entire village. We don't even have electric light. If it weren't for the owners of the Rincón de las Lástimas Ranch who bought a generator, we would live in the dark. They send us a little power we use each night for a couple of hours. It is such a joyful moment when you see the bulb in the kitchen suddenly begin to glow, and you can snuff out those oil lamps with their noxious odor and grayish glow. We'd always rather not light the gas lamp, because then we all suffer. Before doing it, we have to decide to sit absolutely still in one part of the house or on the patio to make sure that the air currents don't break the tube. But it always breaks anyway and then has to be fixed, and we always get blamed. So we prefer to do our chores by the light of oil lamps.

The school here goes only to the third grade. The teacher allows me to attend once in a while so I don't get bored at home and don't forget what I learned in Coyhaique. Sometimes I help him review the first-grade lessons out loud, and outside I teach the bigger kids how to ride a bicycle. My friends have never seen a car. When the bike arrived, they were amazed. It came on an Air Force airplane as a Christmas present for the whole school.

I don't understand the point of living here. Elsewhere you can just go and buy everything at the corner store and listen to the radio to find out what's going on in the world.

Now I'm beginning to realize a lot of things I never even suspected, but the basics still seem pretty unclear.

Julio taught me about life. We spent the winters hunting hares to our hearts' content. Looking back it seems it was all we did, but that can't be true. We would go out after breakfast to check the traps we had set the day before. They were thin wires stretched across the hares' paths, the usual routes they took that we could just make out under the bushes and barbed wire fences. We always found something; sometimes it was even alive. Julio taught me how to kill them quickly so they wouldn't suffer, how to skin them and stake them and many other details I hadn't known before. Together, we hadn't even lived twenty years, but he seemed to know everything. My mother never prohibited this entertainment, and I am sure she preferred it to fishing.

Everything I know about the plants and animals of the south I learned then. We would steal the eggs of the *chur-rete* birds that build their nests on the river banks in deep holes. Julio had a collection of all sizes and colors and strung them like a necklace. We spent our days climbing trees and scrambling through barberry bushes in search of some newborn animal.

Also, during those endless days, he taught me about love.

We were walking along the banks of the Pan de Azúcar, hoping to catch some fish by hand.

"Hey," I asked him, "have you ever been with a woman?"

He didn't pay any attention to me, but I knew he had heard my question. He looked under some rocks and then turned his head and answered grumpily, "No."

We kept searching for victims until he initiated the conversation again.

"I lied," he said. "I was with Maiga the other day, and I touched her tits and other stuff too."

"Where?"

"In the barn. That's the best place to do it. That's my advice, anyway. You invite her to play in the haystacks and then you say you should both hide, and then you start. . . ."

"Maiga? Ema's Maiga?"

"Yep, the very same. What, you think she doesn't like it? Love is something beautiful you have to learn how to do."

I didn't want to reveal my total ignorance of the things he knew and handled with such confidence. We continued talking passionately about the subject.

"Try it," he insisted.

"I don't like it," I said.

Tired of trying their luck in each of the small hamlets of the Aysén province, they decided to stay in Lago Verde. In desperation, they had hiked from Palena, crossing rivers, swamps, and virgin mountains to reach a tiny village they had never even heard of but that, nevertheless, captivated them with its charm, being situated on high slopes that dissolve into the green of the lake.

The strange family immediately became the focus of concern for those who saw in them the beginning of a gypsy invasion. All of their fears seemed justified when Sebastián, the only man in the expedition, erected an enormous orange tent, faded by time and wear, adjacent to the other homesteads in the village, which was growing down toward the lake. What began as a vague anxiety became desperation when one brilliant blue morning, Sebastián began to build the foundation of what would be his permanent house. Even though the family had done no harm to anyone the whole time they had been there, and on the contrary gave every sign of being honorable and hard-working neighbors, the teacher at the school, who was also the judge of the district, could not remain deaf to the complaints being lodged against them. In cooperation with the local sheriff, he summoned Sebastián and his wife.

"People think that if you stay here, the village will be overrun by gypsies. Gypsies and thieves."

Sebastián held his anger in check and remained silent. His wife managed to save him by responding herself.

"Nobody will follow us here," she said. "We are hard-working and honorable people. You can rest assured."

They left the office upset by what they considered to be a foolish and mean-spirited warning. Doña Eduvijes said that she would leave that ungrateful and hypocritical village that very afternoon, that those people should be happy that someone would choose to come live in these parts. Sebastián told her that it was foolish to continue to wander around with two children and that they would encounter problems everywhere because they had been gypsies. While the house was being built and until it was finished, they maintained a strict distance from people who dared doubt the nobility of their customs and generosity. The day they chose to move from the tent to the house, they threw a big party and invited everybody in town. Sebastián himself went from door to door to proffer the invitations. The only people he did not invite personally were the teacher and the sheriff, not so much out of spite, but because he was afraid of another rejection.

But he said again and again and in a loud voice so that everyone would hear, "Everybody come, even those I didn't invite personally."

News of the housewarming party spread beyond the hamlet and reached my father and Moroco in Río Turbio, where they were clearing the fields and forging trails for the animals, and they finally decided to come and meet their new neighbors. To celebrate the occasion in a dignified manner, Sebastián's family had ordered three cartloads of wine from Argentina. They had also arranged for about fifty young lambs and one heifer to be put on the spit. There were many separate fires over a twenty-square-yard area. Some cattle herders arrived, led there by the scent that wafted in all directions and that also attracted a large number of stray dogs that nobody had ever seen before. Everyone ate and drank for two days, and in the house people danced to music played on the RCA Victor with dull, worn-out needles.

Sebastián's two daughters ran around tirelessly to serve

their guests, carrying plates, opening barrels, pouring wine into carafes, and managing to dance with the first ones who grabbed them. That's when everyone found out that the oldest was named Ema and the youngest was Margarita, called Maiga for short. They were thin with light eyes and dull hair, and they looked very much alike. That's when people also realized that there was something strange about Maiga: she spoke very little, didn't respond when asked a question, and walked around laughing with her finger up her nose.

My father went to Moroco and said, "You've got to start thinking about spending the winter in Río Turbio, Moroco."

"What do you mean, don Carlos? You know how high the river rises."

"You will get everything ready ahead of time. We'll spend the coming days supplying the outpost with food and then you can stay there for six months."

"I don't like the idea, don Carlos, believe me, I don't like it."

"But Moroco, remember that I have already invested a lot of money—money that isn't even mine—in those fine cattle we brought from Coyhaique."

"The ones you bought from don Pedro Quintana?"

"Yes. And if somebody doesn't take care of them, they'll die and everything will go to hell, you can be sure of that."

"We'll have to fix up the cabin. Put on a good roof at least."

"Of course we will. But you should start thinking about something else that is just as important."

"And what might that be?"

"Maiga, Moroco. Your Maiga. Talk her into going with you."

"You don't know what she's like, don Carlos."

"At least try. Maybe she'll even like it there."

A flock of sparrows took off flying in a sudden boisterous frolic, spreading a cloak of whispers over the silent space blanketed by oak trees.

When Moroco returned from Coyhaique after completing his military service, Maiga's numerous beaus had to resign themselves to withdrawing their attentions. In the army he had learned, among other things, to give injections of penicillin, a skill that transformed him into a doctor of sorts. In less than a month he had built a shingled two-room cabin, and he set himself up with his aspirin and his medicines. People came from all over to ask him for an injection or help with a birth. They even came to get him from across the border, and he would try to explain that he really didn't know very much, only how to give injections and cure colds and headaches.

"Don't complicate my life with other diseases," he would say.

But people believed more in his healing touch than his knowledge or his medicines and wanted him to come with them anyway, and Moroco had to resign himself to taking his goatskin bag and leaving. Things usually turned out well, until word spread—mean-spirited gossip—that he had been responsible for the death of a good woman whose baby had gotten stuck in her belly. She had lived on the other side of the lake, in an area that was practically inaccessible. By the time they had come to get Moroco, it was already too late. He boarded the boat they brought for him, and when he reached the humble house he encountered a terrible chorus of cries and the owner of the house, nearly insane with suffering.

"We didn't call you sooner, doctor," he said, "because she has given birth so many times with just me to look after her."

Moroco stayed to make arrangements and look after the five children left behind. The wake lasted for an entire night, and then they buried her with her daughter in the green field surrounded by brooklets near the house. Several neighbors came to mourn her. After all that, Moroco returned to the village and heard the gossip and the lies. That is when he swore to limit his doctoring and turn a deaf ear to all entreaties. The first sign of his decision was the notice on the door that proclaimed in bold letters, INJEC-TIONS ONLY. DO NOT INSIST!

That was when Maiga began to visit him regularly. She would arrive early in the morning and remain for the whole day. Those who went to buy something came out saying that she was organizing the shelves and cleaning the bottles of medicines. Those who didn't go in said that she and Moroco were spending the whole day in bed, and that Moroco was attending his patients in his underpants.

Luckily he didn't assign much importance to his clients' giggles; he was just glad that finally they had something to think about. Maiga and Moroco would go out at noon to hunt and would return at nightfall with a string of ducks and great bustards. He was joyful that his life could change without his even hoping for it. That's why he could face the surprise and contempt of the village gossips, who spied from behind their blinds when they realized he wasn't going to pay any attention to them.

Maiga had originally come to his house to ask for pills for a variety of ailments, but he knew that for such imprecise complaints he had nothing to offer. Maiga begged him and Moroco ended up inviting her in to drink *mate* and she accepted. She told him that Ema treated her badly and said she didn't want to go back to her house, not for anything in the world. Moroco almost started crying, suddenly seeing himself there with a real woman of flesh and blood. He showed her how to brush her hair and wash, and he bought her a dress so she could throw out the rags she wore. But she wore it to collect wood, and people laughed at her again when they saw her wearing the new dress, now in tatters, and carrying the logs. Later she explained that she did that because she couldn't stand the shame of looking like the other women of the village, of being as clean as they were. Moroco controlled his anger and bought her another dress.

"They'll get used to seeing you like this," he said.

It was she who let Moroco know that she would be happy to leave the village and never see Ema or anybody in the village again. When Moroco told her about the possibility of going to Río Turbio, she seemed much happier about it than he, who found it difficult to abandon his promising career as a pharmacist.

"We'll go there," she said, "and we'll live happily ever after."

People laughed at them behind their backs. After a few drinks, my father would get on the bandwagon and bad-mouth them as much as the others. Moroco never hid his love from anybody. He hung it out like a flag on Independence Day, and the others would burn their tongues from wagging them so much. They also said that he had gone a bit mad and that it was difficult to know which of them was crazier. We know that Moroco didn't have a foolish hair on his head and that he knew exactly what he was doing. Otherwise he never would have been able to plan that trip with her at exactly the same moment we were wandering around Lago Verde looking for food. He managed to leave one day before us—so we wouldn't be suspected as accomplices—and without anybody knowing where they had gone. We had our suspicions, fearing that Moroco, sick and tired of so much ill will, would take Maiga to Argentina or somewhere else where nobody knew them. Until, that is, we found them on the banks of the lake, waiting for us with a cozy campsite and a hot *mate* to start things off right.

Before bedtime, Moroco called us over to eat. The meat cooking over the juice-covered coals was already browned and gave off a delicious smell. We sat down on the logs around the fire and began passing the slab of meat. My father, who never went anywhere without his knife, was the first to take his share. Then he passed it to Maiga. Moroco cut a chunk and began eating. Then he went to get a bag of bread and passed it around. It was a pleasure to see the way he ate. He held the meat between the thumb and index finger of his left hand and held the bread underneath with the rest of his hand. In his right hand he held the knife he used to cut each bite he took.

With true mastery, he passed it rapidly from his hand to his mouth as he cut each small piece and ate it. I preferred to work on big chunks even if the fat ran down my whole body. The bamboo sticks we used for the rotisserie were stripped bare. Only then did we begin to talk.

"It's because of Maiga that we've only made it this far," Moroco said. "We spent last night here, and today she didn't want to leave until you had arrived."

She was sitting in front of me on the saddle on the ground. From the corner of my eye I managed to see pretty high up her muddy white legs. She didn't seem to care. She took the *mate* and began to drink then handed it to me with a strange expression on her face—almost a smile—that I didn't understand. Then she passed it to Moroco and my father. As she passed it to me again, she said, "Now I'm going to bed."

It surprised us that she went to bed alone, and we didn't know whether this was what she always did or if she was doing so that night out of modesty. Her bed was on one side of the tree, behind ours, and Moroco's was on the other side. After checking to make sure that our horses were securely tied up where we had left them, we also went to bed. We took off only the clothes that were uncomfortable to sleep in, that is, our shoes and jackets. The enormous forest absorbed the darkness, and we could just barely hear the murmurings of the lake. I had the strong sensation that there were, in the quiet, in that nocturnal murmuring, not only our lives but also the lives of many other beings—bees, birds, spiders. I listened to them for a long time with my eyes open, but without seeing anything. When I thought my father was sleeping, I started to get up.

"Where are you going now?" he asked me.

"I'm cold. I'm going to make a cup of coffee."

He mumbled something and turned over. I got up, trying not to make any noise. I stoked the fire and put on some water. The flames lit up Moroco's face, and I saw that he was snoring deeply. I took advantage of the light to look at Maiga and I met her open eyes straight on. I couldn't hide my discomfort, and she smiled. I waited for the flames to die down and slowly approached her.

I sat at the foot of her bed and waited. I could clearly make out the rhythm of her breath, but I was terrified at the thought of somebody waking up and seeing us. I decided to try anyway. Stealthily I moved my hand under her covers until I was touching her legs. I thought that would be the end of it but realized, much to my joy, that instead of that leg jerking violently out of my reach, it moved toward me affectionately. She lifted the covers and pulled me in under them. The sound of our breathing seemed loud enough to awaken all the creatures in the forest. She was wearing nothing under her dress and probably never did. She didn't let me caress her very much beforehand, and she took it upon herself to prepare me so that we would get our work done as quickly as possible. By the dim light from the fire, I could see her face pretty clearly. Her eyes were closed and her face was expressionless and intensely pale. There was neither enthusiasm nor rejection. Her attitude was one of complacence rather than affection, a mixture of indifference and humility. I wanted to remain by her side all night, but after a few moments she gently pushed me out. I scrambled to the edge of the fire where I finished buttoning up my pants. And in order to make sure that everybody knew what I was up to, I went to the lake to get some more water. Then I loudly banged the coffeepot on the rocks near the fire.

When I crawled back into bed by my father's side, he looked at me slyly and said, "How was the coffee?" then pulled up the covers without waiting for an answer.

I am certain that I learned about life during moments such as these and on trips like that. I have clung to my memory of that furtive night in which love was given to me with the same indifference—or naturalness—as food is given. And I took it with the same voracity.

After my encounter with Maiga I had to place a powerful restraint on the thoughts that attempted to grow within me, that tried to dress up real facts with a beauty they never possessed. Maiga taught me to love the same way she taught most of the men in the village, the ones who waited for her in the forest when she went to gather wood or talked to her at night when Ema sent her out to bring water. Leaning against the walls and in dark corners, under the trees or out on the pampa lit by the stars, Maiga got used to making love with generosity and indifference. That's why I felt as if I had suddenly grown up that night.

Many years later, my father would remind me of that night on the banks of the river. And he would say that it was good that I had kept Maiga company, that Moroco, that pig, had left her to sleep alone. It seems that he had planned to do the same thing I had done, but I had beat him to it. I had always thought he believed my story about the coffee. Everything had been so quiet, so synchronized, so dark. Even the banging of the coffeepot on the rocks, so that he would know what I was doing, seemed convincing. But from the very first moment, he knew exactly why I had gotten out of bed.

What I don't know and never will is if Moroco also realized what I was doing and simply didn't care. Having gotten to know him better, I think it might be possible.

Sometimes I see those mountains, those fields, those tree trunks burned black from the fire that raged for ten years, as if through a blurred, almost unreal, image. I feel submerged, buried, as if neither I nor any of that had ever existed. But I know that place is real. I can draw a mental picture of every burned tree trunk lying on every hillside.

It is the same with the people who remained there. Even through a blurred image, they live on in the realm of memory as clearly as I once saw them before me.

And then there are the birds. They continue to follow their arduous paths across the southern skies. And if you have ever observed them carefully, you can never forget them.

The *chucao* is a mysterious bird.

I got to know it as a child when we traveled around the Province of Aysén on horseback, sleeping under the trees, listening to the pitter-patter of rain on the canvas over our heads.

Many of these small birds can be seen on endless treks through areas where they remain free from the daily pursuit of exterminating humans. The *chucao* walks around the forest floor so much that some say he has forgotten how to fly. And since he isn't familiar with people, he thinks they are his friends and wants to hang out with them. He follows travelers around as if he were really interested in them.

The *chucao* has the bad habit of crashing parties. When you are eating around a campfire, its little round yellowish body appears as if to check out what's going on. Then he disappears under the grass and sings, "Chu-caoo."

The people of the region have a lot of respect for this bird. If you are traveling and he sings on your right side, then everything will be okay. But if he sings on the left, the peasants return home and delay their trip until another day.

In spite of his tameness, he is seen only when he wants to be seen. If you hear him singing and go to look for him, you'll never find him. His song seems to vanish and then suddenly is over there then over here, but he cannot be seen anywhere. Perhaps this is why the hunters of Aysén have not managed to exterminate him yet, since otherwise he is such an easy target. Maybe the hunters are afraid he will sing on their left when they are going out to do something important, like catching wild horses, for example.

Even children who go into the fields with their slingshots made of sticks and rubber bands don't shoot these birds. I never shot a *chucao*, never even threw a stone at one, because it would have been like scaring off one's own destiny.

Out there, beyond the mountains of Lago Verde, lives the condor, eating a dead horse in a feast that could last for days.

One unusually brilliant morning, we decided to go to a remote place where those huge birds live. The enormous bird that strikes such a threatening pose on the face of our coins always seemed like a myth, or at most, a distant memory.

The condor is still an aerial presence in this land where the stones and the trees are equally grand. I saw one standing on the head of a dead horse, eating its eyes. All around him, but keeping a safe distance, a wide array of birds of prey such as turkey vultures, hawks, kestrels, and white-throated caracaras grabbed pieces of the animal. They were so focused on their meal that it took a while for them to notice us, at which point they rose to the nearest trees.

The condor lifted his enormous wings covering the horse's cadaver and tried to rise, but couldn't. Even such marvelous wings could not lift such a heavy, satiated body. But he left them wide open: they were white, blue, and black, like a multicolored fan. He looked at us fiercely with his curved beak and bald head. A great necklace of white feathers encircled his neck, making his head look dispro-portionately large.

For one perverse moment we entertained the thought of killing him. I think we were too frightened actually to do it. We waited, watching, until the afternoon. The condor managed to lift himself onto a large boulder and from there jumped onto the branch of a burned oak that groaned loudly under his weight.

Sometimes all I have to do is look at a coin and I travel back to my land, to that afternoon, to stand face-to-face with a defeated condor.

Powerful giant in every feather, but in truth, small, soli-tary, and defenseless.

When spring arrived, the authorities closed the border with Argentina and left us without any supplies. It had been a difficult winter, too long for our stores of food to last. We had all incurred food debts with our neighbors. The authorities were full of explanations and even came to Lago Verde to dish them out. They said they were very sorry, but they couldn't let anybody through, that these were the orders they had received, and they had to carry them out. Things got even more complicated when some people were arrested near the Pico River. They claimed that they had been badly treated. Everything seemed to be working to create an atmosphere of distrust and hostility among the people of the village. And this distrust seemed to be justified by similar problems in other frontier villages such as Pelena and Futaleufú. Right away the police sent a commission to Coyhaique to study the situation, which seemed to be threatening the very existence of the inhabitants of the region. People organized themselves into committees and decided on a course of action. After about two weeks of our passing the remaining food from house to house, an Air Force plane arrived with supplies. It was filled with sacks of flour, sugar, noodles, salt, and even some candy for the children. They dumped the supplies on the airfield, and everyone grabbed what they could. Moments after the airplane arrived, the food was in piles that each group had separated out for itself. One person watched over the merchandise, while another found some way of carrying it away. Julio found a cart, and we got ours home in two trips. Once settled, we were very happy to have supplies again, and my mother immediately set to work making bread. She filled up a bowl and said to me, "Take that to Señora Leonta and tell her we're sorry it took so long for us to return her flour."

Translated by Katherine Silver

—{ Patagonia }—

On the Horse of Dawn

Francisco Coloane

TO PROFESSOR HUMBERTO FUENZALIDA

It passed like a fireball in the distance, expelling something dark and formless under its belly, and stopped only when it got inside the corral.

We all left our lunch in the small dining room of the ranch and ran to see what was happening. Fortunately, it was only the leather straps of the saddle and of some furs that in the crazy race had slipped under the animal's belly. The reins were also split by the trampling, and the foamy sweat showed that the dark chestnut horse had galloped a long way.

FRANCISCO COLOANE *(1910–2002) was born in Quemchi and left school at an early age to begin a life of adventure. He worked in various capacities on sheep farms in Patagonia and Tierra del Fuego, was involved in Chile's first expedition to Antarctica, and was a journalist in Santiago before beginning his literary career. He won the prestigious National Award for Literature in 1964. He has often been called the Jack London of Chile. Francisco Coloane died while this book was in production.*

"Who was riding this horse?" asked Clifton, the second administrator.

"The accountant rode it out this morning," responded Charlie, the *campañistas'* foreman.

"Where to?"

"To Ultima Esperanza and Puerto Consuelo, I think he told me."

"Isn't this Broken Head?" the second inquired, looking the steaming chestnut up and down.

"That's him," Charlie replied.

"And why did you give this animal to the accountant?"

"There was no other . . . the herd had already been released to the open field when he came to look for a horse . . . and I wasn't going to round them up again just for him."

"Why didn't you give him your spare horse and you take this one?"

"Everyone has his own drove of horses—I don't like just anyone going around messing with my horses . . ."

"Mister Handler isn't just anybody . . . he is our accountant, and besides, you gave him this animal out of pure spite, knowing how it came away from its last taming session . . . okay then, leave at once to find out what has happened to the accountant!" Clifton ordered energetically.

"No! I'll go!" I interjected.

I went in to quickly eat some lamb chops, changed the chestnut for another horse that a foreman provided me, and leading it by the halter, I took off on the trail of Alfred Handler, the accountant of the Las Charitas Ranch, located on the southeast shore of Toro Lake in the Patagonic region of Ultima Esperanza.

On the trail I couldn't help but think of how mean it was to have given Handler, the ranch's accountant, an animal like Broken Head, a product of Charlie's last taming. He had been a good horse breaker in other times; but now that he was old and his shoulders and legs had been broken and poorly reset, he broke in horses more with the handle of his whip than with the strap. This is how the chestnut had ended up with that name, precisely because he had broken its skull with whip-handle blows, not being able to break it with his legs. But the most serious thing was that the horse acquired the dangerous habit of rearing and tumbling; that is, he would stand up on two legs and hurl his body backward trying to crush the rider.

The old horse tamer had gone bad not only with the animals but also with his fellow man: every time someone was thrown by a horse a malignant smile blossomed on his lips, and his satisfaction in giving the worst animal to the least expert range rider was poorly disguised.

All this drove me to intervene and look for the accountant; I didn't trust Charlie, who was very capable of taking the same horse and making Handler mount it again just to see him fall another time.

Besides, I liked Handler. He was a man who was too cultivated and delicate for the rough environment of Patagonia, and I had known him in his good times, when he arrived as an assistant to the accountant at the Cerro Guido Ranch. I say his good times, because just as each time the Patagonian lakes run to the sea, their waters become less transparent, Handler's mind was seemingly suffering the same degradation, because of his affection for whisky, some said, or from his readings, with which he became involved for days and weeks, said others. What is for sure is that after having been an excellent accountant at the greatest ranches of La Sociedad Explotadora, he became one at the smallest, our Las Charitas Ranch, with some fifty thousand sheep, and named for the abundance of ostriches that breed on its prairies.

On crossing a streamlet, I could see the fresh tracks of a horse that had come and gone, which convinced me that the accountant had, in fact, traveled toward Puerto Consuelo on the south shore of Ultima Esperanza Bay, where at times he had to deal with business related to shipments of leather and wool. No sooner had I verified the tracks than I spurred the horse and galloped decidedly in that direction with the other horse drawn behind.

The long November afternoon was declining when I saw the rarefied oak woods that characterize the coastal region of Ultima Esperanza and knew that I was approaching Puerto Consuelo.

Little by little the shadows began to wrap up the branches, giving them that impressive animation that trees certainly contain in their sap, but do not succeed in transmitting to their leaves' tranquil palms. I became a little alarmed, not so much because of the nocturnal uncertainty but because I still had not come across any sign of Handler.

Soon the hill appeared, some six-hundred meters high, on whose slope is located the famous Cave of the Mylodon, an opening more or less eighty meters wide, by thirty high, by two hundred deep. On that same southern slope other smaller caves are found, and about three kilometers to the east is one almost half the size of that of the Mylodon.

The place becomes a little strange here, possibly because the fire that destroyed the surrounding oak forests left only black twisted skeletons, at the feet of which new sprouts now appear, dramatically embracing the specters of their ancestors. However, in front of the wide mouth of the Cave of the Mylodon, the fire had kept its distance from a wooded fringe that gave the place the mysterious air of a millennial garden.

I stopped to inspect the surroundings; not finding anything at first sight, I decided to search the smaller caves, beginning with the one located farthest east. With a brief gallop I was at its entrance; I got off my horse and entered it, shouting. I lit some matches, but the shadows were so thick that the light turned back upon me, flashing in my eyes. I went into that hollow as far as I could but found nothing there, either; it was the same in the others of lesser size.

I headed then to the Cave of the Mylodon, ready to examine it more meticulously. Seen from a distance, the oval entrance, with its projecting crags, resembled the big mouth of a great black toad that blended into the body of the night.

Just after entering, after having left the horses tied to an oak tree, I uttered a long shout, calling Handler. Sometimes the sound of your own voice makes you feel safe in the darkness, but this time it would have been better not to have shouted, because a faraway and dreadful shout answered me from deep inside the cave. Steeling my nerves I remembered the phenomenon told to me by some sheepherders who on a day of bad weather had taken refuge there: a person seen at a distance inside the cave seems to be situated hundreds of meters away when he is not more than ten.

Also, some deformation of the voice could occur, returned by the echo through the millennial acoustics, and the hanging stalactites would not be free from that strange effect.

I conquered my fear with another shout, which rebounded less strangely in the hollow of that prehistoric threshold, and this time, after the echo another shout came forth that, even though it made me shiver again, allowed me to recognize in it, full of joy, Handler's voice.

I finally found him in the depths of the cave, behind a low mound of rocks, seated next to a small fire.

"What do you say, Handler!" I shouted to him, stumbling toward him.

"Hey!" he replied, and with a vague gesture invited me to sit down next to him while he scooped up pellets of dry dung to feed the fire.

"I've been looking all over for you," I told him and added anxiously—"has something serious happened to you?"

"I don't know . . . no, nothing . . ." he responded with a voice somewhat detached from reality, with that disturbed quality with which people in dreams speak.

"We were alarmed because your runaway horse arrived at the ranch. . . ."

"It must have escaped, I don't know . . ." he said with that same hollow voice. I looked around, trying to find what I suspected to be the cause of the accountant's strange state; but I couldn't see any liquor bottle. Handler was somewhat dipsomaniac, and sometimes the whiskey brutalized him so much that more than once we found him splashing in the mud formed by the thaw in front of the small dining room; but this time he proved not to have drunk a single drop of alcohol.

The small bonfire continued fighting weakly with the
cave's thick walls, outlining Handler's thin face and making his silhouette dance confusedly on the rocky wall, from
whose roof stalactites hung like huge phantasmal tears. The
accountant was about fifty years old with graying hair; he
was tall, thin, with noble, fine features, a grayish-blue
sparkle in his eyes, and a convulsive grin, somewhere
between kind and sad, on the right side of this thin lips.

"Let's get out of this cave," I told him, gently grabbing
his arm.

"What for?" he replied. "Wait a little bit, I have to tell
you something!"

I sat down next to him with my legs crossed like travelers do when they rest on their heels.

He picked up a good handful of dry dung from the
ground, and then another and another, throwing them on
the fire. It was a very dry manure that didn't seem to be from
either guanacos or horses; it was more like a brown soil, and
its smoke also smelled like burnt earth.

It gave off a sudden radiance and the shadows took
refuge fantastically among the bases of the stalactites; but a
band of dense tatters of shadows began to flutter all around
us, emitting little guttural shrieks as if they were confused
words that sprang from the rock itself. I cowered, seized
with a certain fear, and I confess that I stayed there only
because I saw Handler's impassive expression; he seemed to
receive with pleasure the flapping of those huge black butterflies that screeched like rickety little bellows.

I became calmer when one of those horrible monsters lit
upon Handler's shoulder, and I realized they were bats. The
tiny flying mammal looked at each of us with its tiny black-

ember eyes; it rubbed its little snout like a miniature condor who cleans its beak with the edge of its wing, and it stayed on the accountant's shoulder, blinking at the fire's light; the band again crowded into their nests among the stalactites.

Handler looked at the small animal sitting like a tailless mouse on his shoulder, then at me, with his absent air and his convulsive grin changed into a vague, sad smile. He let his hands drop onto his knees with a skeptical gesture, and he spoke to me with a faraway, lost voice, while he intently watched the fire, as if it were another tongue communicating something to him, half-opening remote shadows of the past.

"It was when the immense cold wave came," he began saying, always in his broken accent. "We still had not learned to articulate; our language was no more than those guttural shrieks of the bats; but we understood each other perfectly, and what the lips did not say, our hands, our eyes, our whole face expressed. . . .

"Of fire, we only knew what the volcanoes belched forth and what from time to time lightning hurled, sowing destruction. But we didn't know how to make it to warm ourselves, and then the cold wave prevented us from living in the meadows, where we would pick greens and catch a sleeping or sick animal or two. Otters and mice were our favorites because we could kill them with stones or sticks, gulping them down raw. Or else we followed the tracks of the great saber-toothed tiger, secretly picking up the carrion that he didn't eat. . . .

"The cold wave pushed us to these woodsy areas. Many of the small animals perished, and the strongest ones also took refuge in the forests. Among them was a small horse, golden like the light of dawn, which at times we corralled in the narrow valleys in order to eat.

"In the meadowlands, women and children belonged to everyone, and all of us cared for them. But when the ice arrived and with it hunger and cold, each man separated with a woman to live alone. I brought my woman to this cave; I put two stakes marking the entrance, and I demolished with a club anyone who crossed the threshold.

"In the sun-filled prairies I used to meet with other men, joining them in cornering some animal; but when the cold wave hit, I took refuge in this cave; I could no longer see other men without hating them.

"Among the animals was one very large one that, like us, ate plant shoots. It had a thick skin covered with scales like little white stones through which red bristles came out like the afternoon sun. When it stood up on its hind paws, leaning on its short, thick tail as if it were another paw, it reached with its long snout to the very heart of the tallest trees, where it found the most tender branches to eat, and in this way seemed to be another, more alive, tree that moved from branch to branch. . . .

"One day I beat one of these large animals with a stick and brought it to the cave. I made a stone fence, enclosing it, and I brought it branches and grass so that it would stay peacefully in captivity. When I got hungry I killed it with club blows, and with the edges of stones I skinned it, carved it up, and ate it raw. I had many flocks of these great animals, one after the other, enclosed in the cave, which I divided into two parts, one for them and the other for my woman and me.

"In that way I held out against the cold wave for quite some time. The woman had a baby, and we wrapped it up with thick furs to keep it warm, but it died from the cold. I made a little niche in the stone, and I buried him so that he could accompany us for a while there. After a short while the woman died too. I made another niche and buried her beside the boy, so that she wouldn't be so alone. . . ."

Handler's voice, like that of a child, was moved to pity and his upper lip began to tremble with cold. Then he raised his hand to his forehead and shielded his eyes from the firelight. The bat was like another small shadow taking shape on his shoulder and only its tiny eyes continued to blink sleepily in the reflections. Then Handler took his hand away from his face and, picking up some more dung, threw it on the flames. They fluttered again, making the shadows dance, and on the wall, on the east side, two open niches could actually be seen; one of the sepulchers was smaller than the other.

"From here," Handler continued, "I could see the great white wave held back on the other shore of the sea's arm; but in reality it was advancing inexorably. From time to time the great wave's crest cracked, launching a deafening thunder, and the ice wore away more of the forest.

"On one occasion in which the thundering increased I headed out, running, in search of other men who might accompany me, but when I approached other caves they came out with their clubs and chased me away just as I had done with them before. Oh, how I missed the gentle look of my woman and the boy's little hand . . . !

"One day the ice thundered so much that the woods filled with shouts, howls, neighing, and the bellowing of frightened animals. I tried to leave the cave, but an avalanche of terrified beasts came this way, along the slope of the hill; many of them followed the hill above, but a group of them, upon seeing the cave's mouth, came in here. I still remember the small golden horse, the color of dawn, that galloped toward that corner, followed by the great saber-toothed tiger and then by the shaggy giant, the swamp otter, and the others.

"Time ran as inexorably as the thundering of the ice, which crumbled like gigantic planks. Animals and birds continued invading hills and woods with their frightened cries. But a colossal stampede resounded more strongly than the others, and the light in the cave grew even dimmer. . . .

"I tried to find courage, but my heart, like a frightened mouse, climbed into my throat. The dim light became condensed between the wall and the stone fence where I had domesticated the large animal . . . and I saw that it was precisely one of them that had darkened the cave, since it had escaped from the enclosure and its gigantic body vacillated, terrorized by the stampede, between entering the cave or running headlong toward the open country.

"Other ashen bodies followed the first, and they began to come down upon me. . . . I fled to the deepest corner of the cave, but the roar of the saber-toothed tiger stopped me. Stuck next to it, the little golden sorrel neighed in terror; but, strangely, the roaring puma made no move to sink its claws into it and eat it up; they were both as frightened as the great swamp otter, which meowed like a bundle of nerves, or as the hairy giant who coughed mutedly, as if it were the throat of the cave itself, stopped up by the fugitive herd. In the midst of the tumult, mixed in with the thundering of the ice, the clear neigh of the little sorrel could be heard like a luminous clarion in the gloomy darkness. . . . .

"Is it the glaciers that rumble? No, because they don't croak that way! It is the ashen body, it is the great animal. . . . His large snout is what croaks and moans that way, subdued like a ruined trumpet from the final judgement. . . . The others also bellow pitifully and they advance, move toward me more rapidly and inexorably than the ice itself. . . .

"Everything is confused: stampede, thunder, roar, swamp otter, cavernous coughing, ululating of the hairy beast, ashes of ice and forest, bird, fish, plants, neighing of the little horse of dawn. . . .

"An enormous paw, yes, an enormous paw . . . ashen, advances and advances until it sinks into my chest. Ay, but suddenly a flash of lightning supervenes! Its light crosses the ancient meadowlands of sun where the plants are juicy and round fruits hang. . . . The flash of lightning flies and in one jagged bolt illuminates all happy life from the past . . . forests that shake like loose hair in a storm . . . I am the tenderest of plants, the sound of water and wind! The wind, the wind, which now uproots me and carries me off through the air. . . . What will become of me? Will I return again to the branch of some tree from which no wind can carry me away? Or will I go away definitively transformed into an errant gust of wind?

"The guttural bellowing, the last neighs of the horse of dawn are fading away, crushed by the ash. . . . The last lightning with its last luminous bolt now liberates the woman . . . from the stone wall she silently slides toward me, as if she wanted to accompany me. She smiles with sadness because she is coming to tell me good-bye. . . . I draw closer and ask her—'How is the boy?' With a vague gesture she responds that he is fine . . . then the boy is okay! But wasn't he dead? How can a dead person be okay? Do they live? Was she dead, too? I approach and graze her ashen smile with my lips . . . how cold they are! They are like the meadows when the ice advanced, like a dead plant. . . . Now I know, she is pretending to be alive! Her smooth, frozen woman flesh is lying! What does she want from me if she is dead? I break away from the ash left by the thunder and lightning, but I don't know where I am going! Perhaps some eternal, errant gust of wind will take me somewhere else where my life can take root again! But if I bloom again will I remember what I lived before? I should! Because if not, it would be better not to resurrect, because oblivion is the only thing that is truly dead."

Handler stopped his disconnected harangue. He looked up at the roof covered with hanging stalactites, as if the entire cavern were crying perpetual, nocturnal, millennial tears. He turned his graying head like a more alive and ashen stalactite, looked for something among the shadows; not finding it, he raised his hand to his forehead again and closed his eyes tightly. The bat stuck out its thin tongue, licked its snout with it, and with the edge of its wing wiped away something like a tiny tear.

"Let's go, Handler!" I said to him, frightening away from his shoulder the little animal who rose up like a humble condor, beating its two little umbrellas of black skin instead of winged plumage.

Outside, the November night was clear and bright. A full moon moved like a great round diamond among cottony clouds, which blended in with the eternal snow of the tall sharp peaks northwest of the gulf of Ultima Esperanza. Up above, the Southern Cross glided toward the Magellan Nebulae; like two gigantic udders they nurtured with milky brilliance that entire portion of the sky.

We mounted up and undertook the return trip to the ranch. We went silently, one behind the other, trusting in the sure gait of our horses. From time to time, in some turn of the road, the moon cast a shadow of Handler's horse, interweaving it with the hoofs of mine.

Past midnight we arrived at the peninsula of Toro Lake, whose point is cut off by perhaps the shortest river in existence: it is only thirty meters long and it joins Maravilla and Toro Lakes together.

Our horses stopped at a stream in a lowland area, where they began to drink. The tops of the oak trees opened up a bit more there, letting the moon shine through, twinkling on the water and the horses' lips, and the water fell like broken crystal when the horses raised their heads to swallow it.

A cloud of mosquitoes rushed upon Handler, and he nervously slapped at his neck, snatching them by the handful. Just then I saw that his hand shined in the moonlight like a bloody limb.

"You're wounded!" I said, coming closer.

"I don't know . . ." he replied, looking at his bloodstained hand.

The mosquitoes insisted on forming a ball at the back of the accountant's neck, and a tiny stream of blood began to trickle down his neck, under his shirt.

"Let me see it," I uttered, spurring my horse.

On the hairy skin at the base of his neck he had a

stanched wound, but with the biting of the mosquitoes and his own slapping he had detached the scab and it was bleeding again. I covered up the wound with a handkerchief to protect it from the mosquitoes, which continued pestering us until we left the wooded area and came to the gentle hills that give way to the open Patagonian pampa.

The lake shore became lower and flatter and treeless, which allowed the silvery light of the water to spread to the pasture with a rare luminosity. This moonlight reflected by the silver plain of the lake and the grassland acquired even more charm when we entered an extensive field of paramelas (*Adesmia boronioides*), shrubs covered with small, thick, yellow flowers, which reached up to the horses' hocks. This paramela along the shores of Toro Lake is a curious plant, with a strong perfume, whose leaves and stems many times replace tea and herb, although they say when you drink too much of it, it produces headaches and hallucinations.

The silver of the lake turned into pure gold when we were right in the middle of the field of paramelas. The blooming bunches, upon being trampled and torn to pieces by our horses' hooves, exhaled their attractive perfume, which was encircling us, just like the golden light that made us imagine we were walking through the meadows of the moon.

Suddenly a group of ostriches got up from the ground— a big male with his five females—and began to run, swerving across the plain with their speckled plumage. Handler kicked his horse with his heels and headed in pursuit of the great birds. Much faster than the horse, they crossed over a hill; at the summit Handler pulled up the reins.

With slow strides I continued waiting for him below, but

on seeing that he remained on the hill like an equestrian statue, I decided patiently to go get him. He was riding a brown sorrel, and when I approached I noted that both man and beast had joined the aura of that night of magical beauty, in which the paramelas gilded the face of the earth with a more vivid light than that reflected by our dead satellite, the moon.

The impressive stillness of the man and beast instilled respect in me. Both of them were enraptured, contemplating the vast landscape. It was as if they had arrived at the end of a long ride and glimpsed the frontier of a spectral world whose border they dared not cross.

In their precipitated escape, the huge birds had raised other groups of ostriches from their nests, and they began to join each other on the side of a nearby hill, observing, curious as always, those who had come to disturb their nocturnal peace.

"How good it is that you have come," Handler suddenly said to me. "Because this way other eyes can contemplate what mine see.

"Because here," he continued, "are the first seven hills that arose from the sea. At that time we still did not exist on the land, and on its shorelines, among algae and grass, were those who were the first to tread upon the meadows from the first mud of the world.

"From the swamps, light rose up in their small brains for the first time, and their thin tongues hit upon the first terrestrial tastes. Naturally they left their huge eggs to hatch in the sun, and then one day the father star cooled off a little, and they did not know how to defend their origins. The eggs did not germinate, and those great species perished."

"What are you talking about?" I asked him.

"You mean you don't see them?"

"Who?"

"The dinosaurs! The dinosaurs!" he exclaimed in jubilation. "There they are on their first hills from the sea!"

"They're ostriches that you flushed from their nests," I informed him, pointing to the great female birds that traveled with gigantic strides on the slope of the other hill, ever hurried along by their huge males whose long, elastic necks moved, undulating like arms that waved meaningful signs at us.

"What a shame that you cannot see what my eyes see!" he replied with sadness.

"Come on, Handler!" I said to him, calmly taking one of his reins and turning him toward the trail that led to the houses of the ranch.

In a while we had begun a good gallop in order to arrive as soon as possible. Upon our leaving behind the country of paramelas and their intoxicating perfume, the violet light that precedes dawn invaded the vast meadows, rapidly displacing the enchanting reflection that the moon was still emitting from the nearness of its setting. Like a slow throbbing, that violaceous splendor passed, and the crude light of dawn plainly revealed all of the contours of the Patagonian landscape. The early morning breeze shook the grasses, awakening them, and a more glorious diamond replaced that of the moon, while horizontally striping the entire earth.

We had just sat down to eat in the small dining room of the ranch, three days later, when we saw Handler suddenly become intensely pale; a sudden trembling shook him, and he collapsed, holding on to the edge of the table.

We all got up to help him so that he wouldn't fall to the floor and, at once, we set him in a chair. The second administrator, somewhat bewildered, quickly tried to open his teeth with a spoon handle and to give him water; but one of the foremen stopped him, warning him that Handler could inhale the liquid and choke.

"His heart is beating," Clifton uttered, after listening to his chest.

In that distant corner of the earth no one could think about a doctor, and so we loosened his clothes and left him in peace.

Three days had passed since the night in which Handler's hallucinations had made me suspicious of his judgment, harmed perhaps by the blow he had received on his head at the base of the cranium. But the strange thing was that during those three days he had carried out in a normal fashion his duties as accountant; of course we never saw him other than at meals, and during them he spoke prudently of routine matters, and he certainly never referred to his accident, nor did he return to his fantastic stories. Neither did any of us allude to his fall from the horse, maintaining the discretion that ranch hands always use in these cases.

"The soup's getting cold!" the second administrator advised, sitting down to serve us from the head of the table, since he was the highest authority there.

Although no one felt like eating lunch in the face of our sick companion's unconsciousness, we sat down, more to accompany our unconcerned second administrator. But our

first mouthfuls of soup were interrupted by a weak moan,
like that of a new calf, from the prostrate accountant.

Little by little the deathly paleness was disappearing and
he came back to life, a gray sparkle beginning to flourish in
his eyes. It was life, and we felt quite relieved after those
long minutes in which we had seen it disappear from our
friend's face.

Handler got halfway up in the armchair and began looking at us one by one as if recognizing us after a long period
of forgetfulness.

"What happened to you?" the second asked.

"The horse threw me . . ." he answered, raising a hand
to the nape of his neck, and while he looked strangely all
around, he added: "But, where am I? I . . . I fell from my
horse in front of the Cave of the Mylodon. . . ."

"That happened on Tuesday and today is Friday," the
second replied, as he stopped slurping his soup.

"What?" Handler asked, surprised.

"You fell off the horse on Tuesday," I interrupted. "The
animal, a runaway, arrived at the ranch and I went to look
for you and found you inside the Cave of the Mylodon. It
was already nighttime when I found you . . . don't you
remember? You were building a fire inside the cave!"

"It can't be . . . I remember that the horse got frightened
by the sight of the cave, reared up on its hind legs, and
hurled me backward. I felt a blow here on my head and
that's all I knew . . . until just now when I woke up thinking that I was still in that same place."

"That happened three days ago," the second insisted; "in
the meantime you have been working in your office and
have come to eat with us every day."

"Working . . . ? Me? In my office?"

"Yes, you."

"No, it can't be. What did I do? What did I say?"

Handler leaned his head to one side as if looking for something that he had left behind. He closed his right eye with a bitter convulsive grin and hid half of his head as if a painful shadow had fallen over it. During those three days he hadn't shaved, and the tip of his graying beard, next to his hair that was now somewhat white, accentuated the impression of a man fallen half way into the past.

"Pardon me," he uttered, "I don't remember anything that has happened to me after falling from the horse."

"It would be better if you ate some warm soup," I told him, when I guessed that the second would insist on knowing more.

But Clifton understood, because when we got up from the table to go to work, he said to me: "Don't go out today, stay in the auxiliary dining room with Handler."

I settled into the small room in the employees' house with the accountant, and it took only one match for the stove, already prepared by the houseboy, to offer us a nice fire. Handler left and returned shortly with a bottle of whisky and two glasses.

"First let's have a drink to clear out the cobwebs," he said, smiling for the first time.

"Thanks," I said, "but it would be good to clear up this mess first and then drink."

"Okay," he said, reluctantly setting aside the bottle and sitting in the other armchair, in front of the stove in whose interior the fire now sparked cordially, "but it seems that it is you who has to clear everything up for me," he added.

"Really, Handler, you don't remember anything about what you have done during these three days?"

"Nothing! I assure you! My last recollection is a kind of difficult tumult that came with the blow to my head upon falling from the horse . . . afterward, nothing, until I began to awaken with a confusing sound of water. It was your voices in the small dining room, and when they became clear, your faces came to me . . . but I swear to you that I thought I'd still find myself on the ground in front of the Cave of the Mylodon."

"And you don't remember the trip we took through the night until dawn?"

"No."

"Nor what you told me."

"No."

"Good grief, they're like three days not lived!"

"Really, during those three days it seems like I haven't lived either!"

"So you mean you were in another world from the moment I found you next to your fire in the Cave of the Mylodon?"

"My fire?"

"You had built a fire with dry dung when I found you, and in its light you told me a strange story."

"Yes, that ground has a meter and a half layer of millennial manure. According to Rodolfo Hauthal, a paleontologist, it came from the *Gripotherium domesticum*, a prehistoric animal that the interglacial man of Patagonia domesticated, enclosing it in that cave as if in a huge stable . . . but what could I have told you about that?"

I narrated to Handler as authentically as I could everything that he had told me, just as I have tried to do now.

"It is simply bizarre what you told me," he said, when I had finished.

"What I have re-told you," I corrected, "since I have done nothing more than return to you your strange story."

"Quite strange!" Handler exclaimed, "but stranger still because in this state of amnesia, caused by the blow to the head, what I told you totally coincides with the excavations that Hauthal did in the Cave of the Mylodon at the end of the last century!

"In effect," he continued, "this researcher found there two empty sepulchers and human remains of the prehistoric man who inhabited Patagonia. These remains were underneath the layer of dung and next to those of four animals until then unknown to science, which pertained to different orders. Judging from the skulls, other bones, and pieces of hide that they found, one of those animals was the size of a rhinoceros and resembled an anteater more than a sloth. Hauthal proved that the troglodyte killed this huge toothless beast, tore it into pieces, and ate it raw, since he still did not know how to use fire. The skulls, which can be seen in the Platte Museum, and the pieces of hide in the ones in Santiago and Punta Arenas reveal that they were killed by club blows and that the primitive man used stone knives to cut up the gigantic animal.

"Lehman-Nitsche and Santiago Roth studied and classified Hauthal's findings, among which were the remains of a gigantic hairy beast, a type of very large armadillo, and a feline that was bigger than all of those known until then.

"But what was most interesting to these men of science were the remains of a small horse, which is now known by the technical denomination of *Onohippidium saldiasi*. They even found the hoofs of this curious animal, one of which still contained the last phalange with its cartilage, and a crown of hairs from its birth. It was a fine coat of a bright yellow color. There is no doubt that this was a remote ancestor of the horse, which became extinct in Patagonia, leaving only that trace . . . that of the horse from the dawn of life!"

"And what do you say about the vision that made you see huge dinosaurs in the common ostriches?" I inquired, now completely captivated by the revelations Handler was making to me through his scientific knowledge.

"Ah," he uttered, as if trying to pry into his memory. "The giant reptiles that in other times dominated all of vast Patagonia, which, as you know, is an ocean bed from which seven geological upthrusts arose! The wise Englishman Huxley made the notable discovery, later confirmed by Scope and other men of science, that these ancient dinosaurs are the intermediaries between certain reptiles and certain birds; these last ones belonged to the same family as the ostrich, the largest of our living birds," the accountant finished, while the fire, although hidden and domesticated between its steel walls, continued fluttering wildly.

Translated by David A. Petreman

Pikinini

José Miguel Varas

I ENJOY OLD WOMEN. I don't mean to say I don't appreciate women of other ages, but the old ones. . . . I say "old" directly, like the Spaniards do, because there's nothing more repulsive than those sugary, slippery, servile euphemisms so much in fashion in Chile: "little old ladies," "golden agers," or bureaucratic formulas like "senior citizen" or "elder adult." Doña Clementina, who was eighty-two with sparse gray hair when I met her, was a remarkable old woman, full of personality and possessed of an exceptional memory.

She had come to Punta Arenas by ship with her mother and four sisters in 1894. Clementina Fidret Bonard was then eighteen years of age. Her family hailed from Dijon, France. Her mother, Jeanne Bonard, was a widow in a difficult economic situation. Drawn by dreams of riches and abundance in the lands of America, plus a few contacts by

JOSÉ MIGUEL VARAS *(1928–) was born in Santiago and is well known as a newspaper and radio journalist. He lived in exile in the Soviet Union for fifteen years during the military dictatorship. Over the last half century, he has published tens of volumes of stories, novels, social commentary, and literary criticism.*

way of family or fellow-countrymen, she had decided to emigrate to Argentina.

Seven tough years in Buenos Aires got her thinking about emigrating again. She was a restless woman, not without some audacity, and tales of quick fortunes being made in the southernmost part of Chile convinced her. So she and her daughters arrived in the city by the Straits of Magellan.

Sixty-four years later, seated in one of those high-backed chairs that the French call *bergères,* in the small sitting room of her house on Calle Bories where she spent most of the day, doña Clementina brought that period at the end of the past century alive.

"When we stepped ashore in Punta Arenas, our hearts sank. We'd been told it was a city where everyone got rich quick. Of course we'd already been told the same about Buenos Aires. In Europe they had a lot of myths about America. Some of them are still around."

The same myth operated farther north in Chiloé, where they reported money thrown away in the streets. The denizens of the straits told the tale of an immigrant from up there in Quellón who, shortly after his arrival, found a ten-peso bill near the docks. He picked it up, but after a moment's thought he dropped it, saying to himself, "The hundreds must be closer to downtown."

Doña Clementina Fidret was a woman with a pleasant face and an intelligent, commanding gaze. Her high forehead made quite an impression, and so did her direct and down-to-earth speech, somewhat brusque and without any sign of hesitation—the speech of someone with strong opinions and no fear of expressing them.

"When your family arrived, Punta Arenas must have been only a small city. . . ." I began.

"City? It would be too much to call it that. There was nothing but a village, and a poor-looking one. We got here at the beginning of winter. The streets were nothing but puddles and mud. Everything was horse-drawn, and the carriages and surreys could barely move; there were only a very few motor cars and trucks. Most of the houses were wooden. In the afternoons the air smelled of damp wood burning in kitchen fires and stoves. Like in Chiloé, the kitchen was the main room of the house. Daily life went on around the stove—that's where you ate and where you lived. Nobody knew about refrigerators or freezers in those days. Because the climate was so cold—and still is—you put meat or any other food you wanted to preserve in a box that stuck out through the walls of the house, with a solid bottom and screens on the top and sides. That's how cold the air was. Even in the hottest summers it didn't get above seventy degrees. In fact, people still store food that way today."

"And the avenues, the plaza, the business district?"

"On one side of the main square of Punta Arenas there was a church, in the same place the cathedral is now. At the center of the plaza was a vacant lot, barren, surrounded by a wooden fence. Somebody—I don't know who—was raising pigs there. Around that space there were some trees. The streets were straight and unpaved. Almost all the houses had fences, stockades. Some of today's important stores were barely more than storerooms, piled high with sheepskins, farm implements, tools, tin washtubs, saddleblankets, sacks of grain, potatoes, *mate*, jugs of wine, and so on."

Doña Clementina said that neither her mother nor she and her sisters had ever imagined how barbaric they would find things here compared to conditions in the civilized and European city of Buenos Aires from which they came. These were the days of the rapid colonization of Tierra del Fuego. Escaped prisoners flooded in, as did anarchists, deserters from faraway armies, adventurers of all nationalities, landless peasants, merchants, ruined entrepreneurs, miners, gold-seekers, ranchers, and legions of vagrant prostitutes.

At that time land grants were available in Tierra del Fuego, but at first not many people were interested. Settlers must have been afraid of the Onas, the primitive inhabitants of the Big Island. Legends were told of their savagery, and there was also talk of the savagery of Jules Popper's men, dedicated to the task of killing them. One of the leading Indian-killers was a Scotsman, Alex MacLenan, otherwise known as the Red Pig. He had installed a long pole, a sort of pike, in front of his house in Tierra del Fuego and would impale the head of an Indian on it. It was said he replaced the head every day.

These were the days of the "white guanaco" that Francisco Coloane has brought to life in a novel and various stories. The *Selknam*, tall and striking primitive inhabitants of Tierra del Fuego, also known as Onas, survived mainly by hunting guanacos. They ate guanaco meat and used the hides to cover themselves during the colder months. The white colonizers began to fence in the land and raise sheep, taking advantage of the rich natural prairies of the Big Island. They massacred guanacos at such a rate that the

Onas began to go hungry, traveling a long way to find even one animal at a time. Under those conditions, and lacking any notion of private property, they began to kill and eat sheep, the white guanacos.

The big ranchers, meanwhile, had gradually been putting together armed bands, groups of men supplied with carbines or rifles, and sometimes with military training by European mercenaries. Their mission was to protect the fenced-in fields and to eliminate marauding pumas that would devour the sheep. They were paid one pound sterling per puma on presenting the skin of the animal as proof.

But the hunt soon turned toward human prey, the Onas, who were considered marauders as well. The reward per corpse was the same. At first the hunters presented the two ears of a *Selknam* as proof of death. When a captain noticed how many natives were going around without ears, however, the requirement for payment was changed to the entire head.

Doña Clementina said that word had begun to circulate in Punta Arenas about a terrible massacre that the ranchers' armed bands had committed in Tierra del Fuego.

"Many people justified the extermination, saying that the Indians ate up the sheep and couldn't understand they weren't supposed to. A day or two later, there was a tremendous commotion in the town."

The whole city turned out on the streets to watch the triumphant armed force and its prisoners go by. It was the private army of Mauricio Braun, and the prisoners were mostly women and children. One hundred and sixty-five in all, but no one knew the exact number until later. Many of the women had little children in their arms. The bigger children, from five to nine years old, walked on their own.

My conversation with doña Clementina Fidret took place in early winter of 1958, a year of interminable snowfall to the point where airplane service was called off. The flat roofs of sheds collapsed under the weight of accumulated snow, as did those of some modern California-style houses poorly adapted to Punta Arenas. On the steep slope of Calle Roca, across from the offices of the Society for the Exploitation of Tierra del Fuego (which decided, years later, to change its name), it was nearly impossible to avoid slipping and falling. The snow had turned to polished ice. The staff of Radio La Voz del Sur would climb out on the roof to shovel the snow, and the street was a narrow passageway between two white walls.

But that afternoon the sitting room in Calle Bories was very hot, and I had to remove not only my overcoat but— with doña Clementina's permission—my jacket as well. So it came naturally for me to ask her whether that parade of Ona prisoners had taken place in winter or summer.

She remembered it very well:

"It was winter. I think it was July . . . yes, July of 1895. People said later that it had been the coldest winter of the century. Something like thirteen below zero, if I remember right."

"Legend says that the *Selknam* were very resistant to cold."

"That's true, but there are limits. They went naked most of the year, and in the winter they wore guanaco hides. But the hunters had taken away the hides from the ones they forced to walk in that procession and given them scraps of clothing, ripped up coats or jackets, and some dirty blankets instead. You could see that everyone was half-dead from hunger and cold. They were all barefoot. Some of them could hardly walk. I think some of them were wounded. Señor Braun's brave mercenaries paraded them before the townspeople, maybe with the idea of celebrating their victory, which meant the extermination of almost all the Onas—the end of a long campaign."

"And what was the reaction of the people watching this parade?"

"There was some applause, it's true, maybe from the ranchers or the people who worked for them, but not much. Most people there felt shame and pity, especially for the mothers and children. Some women cried."

Doña Clementina remained pensive and didn't speak. She offered tea and homemade cookies, which her great-niece Adriana Perrière served.

"Excuse my persistence, but what you're telling me is so. . . . What was done with them afterward? With the *Selknam* prisoners, I mean."

"They put them in a sort of shed with no roof. They kept them there, shut in, in that incredible cold. None of this was secret, because the Indian hunters thought what they had done was—how shall I say it—meritorious. The young people and many of us children crowded up to that windowless wooden corral to try and see something. All sorts of rumors were circulating. Later we found out that the organizers of the massacre, trying to make something from it any way they could, began to sell the Ona children."

"Sell them? As slaves?"

"I don't think that word was used. It seems there was no lack of takers. Some well-off people of Punta Arenas found children a good investment. Labor was scarce in those days. Men of working age came to get rich or, at least, to find a job with pay that made up for the climate and the distance they'd come. Some left to prospect for gold in Tierra del Fuego. Others hired themselves out as shepherds, cowhands, shearers, or horse trainers in the ranches of Patagonia, whether Chile or Argentina. The conditions were similar on both sides of the border, and the ranchers came from the same families."

"So, men were scarce in Punta Arenas. . . ."

"Only up to a point, because others kept emigrating from Chiloé or arriving in ships from other lands. But also, there weren't many women to do domestic tasks. Many were sought after or already contracted by the white-slave rings. In a land of single men, there was demand for them. Others got married."

"And so?"

"To have a 'little Indian' in the house could be a good thing. Sure, you had to raise them and clothe them and feed them, but then they'd chop wood, sweep, take care of the pigs, help with the household chores, maybe even cook. That was the fate of a good number of children. But when those brutes began to take them away, sometimes tearing the littlest ones from their mothers' arms, the *Selknam* women rose up. It was their great rebellion. I don't know all the details, but they fought their way out of that prison— I don't know how—and ran through the streets searching for their children and crying out, '*Pikinini . . . pikinini.*'"

"What does that word mean?"

"I don't know. Maybe that was what little ones were called in their language. Or it's what they thought they heard being said in Spanish. A dozen or more of these women, mad with pain and despair, broke the windows of a butcher shop—or that's what people who saw it say—and made gashes in their arms and breasts with the points of the broken glass. They ran, waving their arms dripping blood and showing their bleeding breasts while they cried out in their sharp voices, '*Pikinini . . . pikinini.*'"

The conversation waned. Doña Clementina Fidret was very quiet. Her great-niece seemed about to cry. No comment was needed, or possible. We drank a second or third cup of tea. I said good-bye and wrapped myself in my coat, knotting the thick woolen scarf around my neck, putting on my gloves, and pulling my beret down over my head.

I went down the stairs barely able to see where I was going. It was nighttime, though not quite six in the afternoon. My footsteps made a harsh, rough sound on the dark path of trampled snow that other walkers had engraved on the street. While I walked toward Calle Lautaro Navarro, I thought I heard a faraway echo, *pikinini . . . pikinini.*

Translated by Dick Cluster

A Lone Horseman

Patricio Manns

THE ARROW FLEW from autumn to autumn and quivered as it pierced the horse between the eyes. The horse was black. The white, shaggy star on his forehead was, indeed, an easy target: it could be seen from afar, even when shadows resided in the space that separated the observer from that glowing point of reference. The horse could always be found behind it, attached to this imprecise tattoo with its five improbable points. First the animal heard the whistle as it approached. Then the arrow embedded itself

PATRICIO MANNS *(1937–) was born in the Bío-Bío region of Chile and lived in France for many years after the military dictatorship took power in Chile. He has written dozens of novels, testimonials, and volumes of short stories, essays, and poetry and won countless prizes in Chile and internationally. He was one of the most important members of the New Chilean Song Movement and continues to perform and compose extensively. His novel* Corazón a Contraluz *from which this text is taken, is a fictionalized biography of Jules Popper, the Romanian Jew and notorious gold digger, entrepreneur, explorer, historiographer, and Indian-killer who lived in Tierra del Fuego at the end of the nineteenth century. The novel was published in French and Spanish in 1976.*

with precision and with violence, and a slow stream of
blood methodically erased the star. The horse reared, its
front hooves flailing in the air. An instant later, the rider
wailed and grabbed the bridle. The arrow had also perfo-
rated the shifting shadow of his deliberations.

Maneuvering carefully inside the curved twilight, anoint-
ed by the tenuous spray of the sun that was setting, sizzling,
into the ocean behind the mountains, he reached out his
arm until his hand rested on the trembling neck, a pulsat-
ing neck drenched in sweat and fear. His fingers sought
gently, compassionately, soothingly. A moment later they
encountered the cruel hardness of the arrow buried in the
hide and partially embedded in the bone of the forehead
between the two black eyes that burned with terror. The
horseman's hand had a mind of its own, for his eyes were
searching separately and with absolute concentration
around the spot where wooden bolt and its small spur of
stone—or rather silex—had taken off in search of his chest.
He tensed his arm and yanked out the foreign body that
had briefly transformed the jet black horse into a unicorn.
The horse reared and again clawed at the wind with his
front hooves. He was overcome by pain, and his nostrils
dilated as he neighed his confusion, his attempt to understand the reason for this second torture, inflicted this time
by his own rider.

The horseman spurred the horse, loosened the reins, and
galloped away from a knoll he had just noticed on his right.
A wide shadow advanced from the foot of the Carmen
Sylva mountain range and crept gloomily, threateningly
over the expansive tundra. A hundred yards away he dis-
mounted and threw the reins over the wounded head and

onto the ground. The horse shook anxiously. His trembling lips were covered in foam. The rider pulled his head toward him and kissed him tenderly. He examined with his eyes and his fingers the point of impact: a viscous halo had spread precisely over the middle of the star that shone on the horse's forehead. The wound, however, was not deep.

"Your head is made of iron, Moloch," he said out loud. He cleaned the wound, examined it, and cleaned it again, adding, "I am in your debt. If you hadn't reared up and positioned your head where you did, that arrow would have pierced my complicated heart."

He said "complicated heart" with such naturalness that the horse, from his vantage point behind the wound, dismissed any suspicion of rhetorical pretensions. Nonetheless, he contracted his buttocks and expelled a quivering flood of steaming excrement, further dilating his suspicious nostrils. The thin blanket of bluish shadows was now joined by scattered black cumulus clouds, but to the west, a rose-colored light still floated across the lower half of the sky. There was almost total silence: only the distant shouts of sea birds, the swish of the wind rolling over the tundra, and the scraping of hooves on the ground kept it from being absolute. The rider's boots hung loosely on either side of the saddle, and his gloved hands pulled a Remington out of its holster.

"We're going to defend ourselves," warned the man under attack. "Don't move and don't say anything."

He shot twice, consecutively. The detonations shook the entire landscape. A wild goose shot into the air from the grass, screeching in terror, piercing the cottony sky like a well-aimed arrow. Then a calm laden with omens settled into the space between all action and all sound.

Horse and rider continued across the tundra, always keeping their distance from the high tongues of flame that rose, here and there, from the earth. They advanced in the center of a vast, moving sphere. Such a sphere is, of course, an optical illusion in this flat landscape of Tierra del Fuego or, as he preferred to say with more precision, it is a minor example of Fata Morgana's influence. The sphere moved across the entire afternoon in the company of the horse and rider, having incorporated them into its isochronal, progressive, oscillating rhythm, and the pasture's shaggy softness drowned out the sound of the pounding hooves. The horse's shadow oscillated and the rider's shadow oscillated too, a hazy knight backlit by flames. The absence of other footprints carried them along a fixed azimuth that led toward the eastern horizon, a specific point along this semicircular and slightly warped line: the horizon of both the high seas and the flatlands. Because wherever one goes, so goes the circle, stretching out behind the flanks of the horse or the ship, to port and to starboard of the horse and the ship, only to meet, finally, far away, behind, beyond the haunches, to the stern of the traveler. The line merged, held, dissolved, only rarely broken by hillocks and sporadic rises. Only under exceptional circumstances will surroundings such as these adopt some shape other than this discouraging circle, pure yet firm, which offers nothing to the eyes of those who seek a physical point of reference to guide them, who must eventually resign themselves to the totality of the tundra, unfurled, by twilight or daylight, devoid of trees and large bushes and brutally assaulted by the habitual activity of the perpetual winds. From the girth of the horizon he had just left to the girth of the horizon he was approaching, the horse obeyed his rider. The horseman's eyes never stopped scanning the infinite savanna covered with dense, short thickets of broom sedge; in certain spots there were thickets of an unusual black shrub (though black be the absence of color), and in others, small lagoons floated on the surface of the earth, like lidless eyes enigmatically watching the turn of events in the quicksilver of the cloudy sky.

He had to stop often to allow his eyes to search as far as they could see, looking for any sign of his attacker, but only the grass waved. Across the small rises, along the forsaken edges of the lagoons, behind the dry shrubs, into the slight depressions that suddenly break the monotony of these grass-covered flatlands, his eyes found nothing. At a particular moment he impatiently pulled on the reins and grabbed the horse by its bridle so that he could look more carefully. He did so not as a routine part of his vigil but rather because he had perceived a nervous tremor running through his saddle, felt the horse's rapid and agitated breath. From under the visor of his fur cap, his hard blue eyes quickly scanned the landscape tinged with the reflection of the orange aureole, methodically sweeping over everything in sight; in spite of the penetrating intensity of their gaze, they saw nothing extraordinary. (When a solitary traveler searches the lonely tundra, he seeks the extraordinary.) The wind that blew from the other sea—he was approaching one sea and leaving another behind—hit him in his face that was burnt by the glare of the sun, the drag of the whirlwind, the rash ray, the earth in grisaille, the yeasty sea foam frothing in the waves along the coast. He shook out his frame, his wide shoulders, his gloved hands.

Then he shook his purplish hair that stuck out from under his cap, his large white ears strung with small blue veins, his wide forehead, his face with its vigilant expression, both impassive and cruel; his eyes were so keenly focused that his other senses seemed impervious to all save the thin scent of the salty sea soaked with iodine that may have reached his nostrils.

He exclaimed with satisfaction as he crossed his leg over the stirrup. The remaining light lingered in the air, but the night was already gathering its heavy belongings in all the empty space, and time, forcing the night to mature quickly, hastened the night's solid descent to earth. In these latitudes, as the sun sets, the crest of the mountain range tosses its shadow over the eastern shore—for there is also a western shore—and the light remains, reverberating over the agitated surface of this, the last ocean. The flames of Tierra del Fuego, scattered over the tundra and even approaching the spur of the mountains, stood out more visibly.

~

In spite of the gunshots, there was no sign of life from the mound. No sign of death either. For a few minutes, with his knee on the ground, the horseman observed without blinking and made his calculations. He must have seen nearby the heap of grass and bits and pieces of black brush, cut and arranged to provide cover for a man and allow him to fire freely. This is how the Fuegians had stalked their prey since before the official birth of memory in Tierra del Fuego. The guanacos, the ostriches, the bustards were all hunted this way. The arrow came from there. The hideout, built in haste with bundles of small twigs and dead leaves, was very flimsy. (This can be clearly seen in many of the photographs he took at this time.) It was obvious to the rider contemplating it that the use of more solid materials, such as stone or wood, would have made it less vulnerable. He took aim and pulled the trigger for the third time. He had focused his assault on this spot, yet because of the lack of any sign of life he remained, undoubtedly, rather perplexed.

"So Moloch, what do you think?" He lifted his eyes to the horse's. He placed a handful of dry grass on top of his cap to find the direction the wind was blowing and added, "That bastard must have caught at least one lead splinter. Come on, let's go see."

He stood up tall, pulled the visor down over his forehead, lifted himself into the saddle, and pushed his heels against the horse's flanks. He tried to approach the grave mound, but the horse dilated its nostrils and snorted, assaulted by a nameless terror. The rider held on to the reins with his right knee, thereby freeing both hands for the Remington. The centaur advanced some twenty yards, then stopped to watch and listen. In the heart of the steppe all sound again appeared to have died.

"You see," he whispered, "we got him. Never again will he attack a traveler with impunity."

He barely had time to throw himself down against the mane on Moloch's neck when the second arrow flew toward him without a single movement, the shadow of a hand, or the slightest shiver of a hidden, tensed arm to warn him of an attack. The horse again reared on its hind legs, preventing the rider from immediately returning his lead response.

"Down, you fool!" he shouted striking the horse's confused head with the butt of the gun.

The horse's lips were covered with gray froth, and its
muffled neighs sounded like sobs. Again they were beyond
the deadly reach of the archer. The face of the man under
attack, frozen into an arrogant and rigid mask with a secretive grimace that might well have risen from the depths of
his being or from the bitter consciousness of his own vul-
nerability, now looked deeply lined and darkened.

"Listen carefully," he said, as usual talking to his horse.
"I've got a lot at stake in this game. I must hurry up and
force that felon to play all his cards out there on the grass."

The attacker's small mound formed the center of a relief
of barren, porous rocks, washed by the rain and worn down
by the constant assault of the four winds: the white wind
that clambered up from the south, the green wind that blew
in from the Atlantic, the blue wind that grew stronger as it
crossed over the Pacific, and the black wind that hailed
from the north. The gray spikes of the broom sedge, the
grass-plant of the Patagonian and Fuegian tundra that is
stiff and stubby like a dwarf bulrush, grew in the interstices
and was therefore called by the native people an interstitial
plant. When young and tender, it quickly and consistently
filled the interstices of bovine, equine, and ovine hunger.
Whoever was hiding in that mound had an excellent view
of the entire area and would be able to prevent a surprise
attack. Equally, however, it would be impossible for him to
escape without being seen and, more importantly, shot. His
actions were presumptuous as well as fatal.

The horseman's brain was most likely working with cold

efficiency. As far as an eventual siege was concerned, the absence of rocks or significant depressions in the earth precluded a covered advance. By the same token, he surely understood that the invisible archer was completely blockaded: once he had used up his arrows, he had no choice but to emerge abruptly and engage in hand-to-hand combat. Even this was impossible: the horse and the Remington were enough to nullify this option. The man on the horse knew then that his only problem was to force the quickest possible exhaustion of his attacker's quiver, even if it meant taking the risk of receiving, at any moment, a wound of incalculable consequence. The two projectiles that had already been shot at him could have killed him or led to injuries that would cause his death.

"But I have an idea." He directed his thoughts out loud to his horse. "Do you know why his shots are so strong and well guided? Because the rogue is counting on the wind, because he is using the wind like a river to quickly carry the arrows straight to us. That means we should attack from the other side. Then his arrows will be weakened the moment they leave his bow; they will fly off course and lose their accursed magic."

The black horse broke into a gallop, tracing a much wider circle that kept them beyond the reach of the bow, though from their new vantage point, they could not see their enemy. This thought made the rider spit with icy rage and wipe his lips on the back of his gloves.

"Open your eyes wide, Moloch," he said, perhaps unnerved by this realization, while he gently rubbed the neck of his hairy companion, "because it is obvious that this human scum is learning. If that conniving bastard," and he pointed with an accusatory finger, "had the proper tools, he would dig a trench, a pit, a hideout that would be much safer." His eyes wandered, then focused on something in the distance. He mumbled, "His cave made of plants is a joke, but such as it is, it almost killed us. If he had discovered the right tools just fifty years ago, his race would still be alive and thriving. His whole race will now be exterminated. That is why I am doubly obliged to kill him: he was born with eyes and memory, something always dangerous in a man like him, so close to a beast. Do you hear me?" he asked the horse. Then changing his tone, his intention, his mood, he fixed his eyes on the mound, and his shout exploded simultaneously from his hardened lips and the silent landscape: "Now show me your horrible animal face so I can blow it to pieces."

He aimed his gun and fired. The shots stirred up small spirals of grass. He descended from his bucking horse and, like a cautious and civilized knight, rested his right knee on a patch of damp gravel while he reloaded his gun. Later he would claim that he had felt the humidity in the ground through his knee, for it was still soaked from the last rains. During the course of a normal year, there are days of rain, days of snow, days of ashen shrouds that push a powerful wind the indigenous people call "Walaway," and days of sun, the southern sun covered and uncovered by billowing untamed clouds. He would also say that medallions of dark mud, kneaded by the recent rains, shone through the trampled yellow grass. He aimed and fired. He slithered along the ground for a dozen yards, transformed by malice. He raised his torso to take aim, the shot rang out, and he threw himself down again, all with much physical agility and no sign of scruples; never would he accept that the best way to end this battle was to get on his horse and ride away. In spite of everything, the third arrow never came.

"Are you dead?" he shouted.

There is no echo in the tundra. Echoes are the inventions of mountains and cliffs. For this reason, solitude in the tundra is especially eloquent, though at this moment the shooter, in his agitation, had no time to appreciate it. His eyes shone with the danger and clamor of battle. Moving his left arm, he opened the zipper on his pants and let out a stream of throbbing urine, hot, restless urine that fell to the ground like a jet of yellow dewdrops, ill-timed and steaming. He closed the zipper, repositioned his arms, turned his head around to look over his shoulder, and shouted so the horse would hear him, "Last round!"

He pressed the trigger several times, dragging himself along the ground to fire from different angles. He kept shooting for some time, and would have continued had he not seen the inert open hand, palm facing the darkened clouds, barely visible on the indifferent weeds of the vulnerable hideout. At first he thought that this was but a primitive phantom wedged between the rough stones, and for a whole minute he held his breath and looked at the hand without blinking. Moloch saw it too. Fascinated, suspicious, and standing tensely on his four shaking legs, he couldn't resist the temptation: he approached the body fearfully, caught a whiff of the mysterious significance of this nearly transparent secret presence, snuffed out on the earth, a broken human existence stretched out, chaste and impenetrable. With ceremony, the hardened seducer of death put down his Remington, pulled out a silk handkerchief with the initials "I.P." embroidered on it, and wiped his ungloved, satisfied, fearsome hands, then walked over to the dead man. In the semidarkness imbued with otherworldly emanations, a vibrant red brush stroke now lit up the sky, getting suddenly brighter toward the northeast.

"Why did you attack me?" he asked politely. "My horse and I were passing by with tranquil hearts and a tired step after a long day of work and you shot us, without any warning, with your pathetic shower of two arrows."

He raised his handkerchief to his lips as if it were a linen goblet and wiped them off. He also cleaned off his right boot by rubbing it against the left. He unbuttoned his rugged lambskin jacket.

"I don't understand."

It could be said he looked pensive, as if he were truly engaged in a deep exploration of the intricacies of aboriginal behavior, an attempt to find palpable proof of atavistic, evil impulses. "Did you really think you could kill me with two arrows? Because you only shot two arrows at us. You have none left in your quiver, and I carefully counted. Have you ever heard of such a thing?" he asked, turning slightly toward the horse. He sighed and sat down on the ground next to the corpse of the adolescent boy. At the same time, and with the same movement, he stretched out his seven-league boots. He was slowly recovering his composure. He touched the first wound—there were two— with his fingertips, dipping them in the warm blood, and smiled. The bullet had entered through the left clavicle, vertically, as if it had been shot from outer space into a man standing up, and zigzagged downward until it pierced an artery in the Indian heart, devastating everything in its path. Then it exited by breaking through several ribs level with the right elbow. Perhaps the bullet had hit its mark while the besieged archer was curled up on the ground, trying to dodge the bullets that flew around him.

"Idiot," the other muttered, even more passively, "what did you think you could do against a horse and a Remington? What could your miserable bow do against our speed and our technology? Throughout the entire Fuegian region, I represent the power of technology that is otherwise unknown in this quadrant of the world, but your dim brain didn't understand anything. If you had wanted to save yourself, all you had to do was ally yourself with me, not fight against me. Only by my side would you stay alive and keep your race alive, but you belong to the last remnants of a people resigned to extinction. With the abolition of slavery, your race has no reason to exist, it has no further mission to accomplish. As far as the extinction of your blood goes, there is no alternative: nobody can abolish death."

The young body lay on its back: its legs were spread, its arms crossed, its eyes wide open, its hair tangled and stiff, its lips pressed together, its chest concave, its belly sunken, its ribs protruding, its navel full of the only piece of earth that was left to it; it had scratched knees, a pained expression, a dark, dull nakedness that was also absolute, compact, primitive, naïve. The bow also lay dead next to the left hand.

"In spite of all that, you were beautiful, a young and beautiful hunter with easy arrows."

With a sudden impulse, he reached out his hand and touched the forehead. From there his hand descended, tracing a long line down the check, the hairless chest, the belly, until it ended its voyage on the sex, also lying at the foot of its own curly bush. His fingers tightened tenderly around it, with moist harmony, transfigured by a benevolent guttural current that may have flowed from the deep, shady corners of this knightly heart. When the black horse suddenly snorted, his master lifted his eyes, surprised at being surprised, and was brought back to the splendid cold evening that followed the battle. He scrutinized the horse's eyes and said in subtle warning, "You have seen nothing, Moloch."

He scratched his chest through his jacket and added, "Anyway you were looking toward El Páramo, and you can't see in two directions at once."

The horse pawed the ground with his front hooves. He shook out his mane. Suddenly, he snorted again when a silhouette sketched itself against the grave mound. The scowling horseman turned to look and astonishment spread over his face: a naked adolescent girl stood staring at him without moving. He could tell she was adolescent by the size of her newly born breasts and short, curly, and scarce pubic hairs. Her face belonged to a beautiful dark-skinned fifteen-year-old, but she had white hair. They stared at each other for a long time. The horseman stretched out his hand to her, but still she did not move. He touched her white hair in disbelief—she saw his incredulity and lived to describe it. He seemed to be admiring her slender body and her height, for her large eyes stared at him from just below his own, and he was a very tall man. He went to get a blanket from the black horse's haunches and covered her with it. He mounted, picked her up from the ground, and seated her astride the saddle, facing him, allowing her to press up against his belly and wrap her arms around his waist, burying her white head in his pounding chest. The silhouette of the man against the dusk, distorted by the shadows of the tongues of fire that rose irrepressibly from the deep purple earth, moved forward slightly and, hanging from the reins, bent over to pick up the Remington. It slipped into its holster like a long finger penetrating a glove. Then he galloped a fair distance until night had fallen and he had reached the upper edge of a cliff. The whole way he felt the warm skin of the adolescent girl. He made his way down a path of good fortune until he reached sea level. From there he could see his fort, El Páramo, and make out the shadows of his men against the darkness. He crossed the gateway at a slow walk. The silhouette of the guard saluted him and said, "Got some fresh meat, Captain Popper?"

And without a moment's hesitation, he responded, "Nobody will touch her, Absalón. If I find out that anybody is dreaming about her, either awake or asleep, I'll shoot him."

Translated by Katherine Silver

Translators

KATHERINE SILVER (1957–) is a freelance translator, editor, teacher, and writer who has lived in Chile frequently and for long periods from 1979 to the present. She has translated the works of Antonio Skármeta (*The Postman*), Elena Poniatowska, José Emilio Pacheco, and Martín Adán. She has also translated Pedro Lemebel's *The Queen of the Corner* for Grove/Atlantic Press (2003).

~

DICK CLUSTER is the author of the novels *Return to Sender, Repulse Monkey,* and *Obligations of the Bone.* His translation from Spanish has focused especially on Cuban writers, including story collections, novels, and anthologized stories by Aida Bahr, Alejandro Hernández Díaz, Pedro de Jesús, Antonio José Ponte, Abel Prieto, Mylene Fernández, and Mirta Yáñez.

LISA DILLMAN is a Lecturer in Spanish at Emory University in Atlanta. She has translated biography, art history, and pedagogy in addition to Spanish, Catalan, Cuban, and Argentinian fiction. She is the co-editor with Peter Bush of *Spain: A Traveler's Literary Companion.* Her most recent translation is the novel *Pot Pourri: Whistlings of a Vagabond,* by Eugenio Cambaceres (Oxford University Press).

NANCY ABRAHAM HALL has been a member of the Wellesley College Spanish Department since 1989. Raised in a bilingual household in Mexico City, she holds a Ph.D. in Hispanic American Literature from Harvard University. Her most recent publications include articles on Borges, Boullosa, and Fuentes. Currently she is co-editing *Studies in Honor of Enrique Anderson Imbert (Juan de la Cuesta)* with Lanin A. Gyurko of the University of Arizona.

ALFRED MACADAM is the editor of *Review: Latin American Literature and Arts,* a publication of the Americas Society. He teaches Latin American literature at Barnard College and Columbia University. He has translated Carlos Fuentes, Mario Vargas Llosa, Julio Cortázar, and other Spanish American authors.

DAVID PETREMAN is currently a professor of Spanish and Latin American literature at Wright State University. He has published books and articles on Latin American literature and his poetry can be found in many U.S. and Canadian literary journals. He has translated the work of a number of Chilean writers and poets. His most recent book is *The Faces of Rain (Los rostros de la lluvia),* a bilingual edition of the poetry of Marino Muñoz Lagos.

HARDIE ST. MARTIN has translated work by Vincente Aleixandre, Roque Dalton, Enrique Lihn, Nicanor Parra, and Luisa Valenzuela, among others. He is the recipient of a number of fellowships and awards, including a John Simon Guggenheim fellowship in 1965, and a P.E.N. International Translation Award and an ALTA award for excellence in editing and translation. He lives in Barcelona.